The Unsinkable Heather Mills

THE UNAUTHORIZED BIOGRAPHY
OF THE GREAT PRETENDER

NEIL SIMPSON

PHOENIX BOOKS

The opinions expressed in this book are those of the author of this book
and do not necessarily reflect the views of the publisher or its affiliates.

ISBN: 1-59777-557-6
Library of Congress Cataloging-In-Publication Data Available

Book Design by: Sonia Fiore

Printed in the United States of America

Phoenix Books, Inc.
9465 Wilshire Boulevard, Suite 315
Beverly Hills, CA 90212

10 9 8 7 6 5 4 3 2 1

Hitting the Floor

Heather Mills stood poised at the base of the gleaming golden staircase. She was standing on a Hollywood soundstage, taking the biggest gamble of her extraordinary, high-stakes life. More than 400 people in the *Dancing with the Stars* studio were watching open-mouthed and 22 million more fans were glued to their TV screens at home. Everyone wanted to see if this scandalous British beauty could achieve the unimaginable. She forced herself to smile as the studio went quiet. She wasn't going to disappoint them.

Watch the one-legged girl do the samba, she thought wryly. *I'm going to put on the show of my life.*

But in the last few moments before the music played Heather nearly lost her nerve. She was terrified. Her eyes flicked to dance partner Jonathan Roberts, standing motionless at the base of the second set of steps. He was still as a statue, looking down at his feet and getting into character. Jonathan always looked so cool. Was he scared, too? Probably not. Nervous perhaps. But she knew he didn't have as much to lose as her. He didn't have as much to prove.

The silence seemed to go on and on. Heather waited for that first crashing chord—her signal to dance, to compete, to win. She went inside herself, as she always did in the bad moments. She searched for positive thoughts to give her strength.

I know I look bloody good, she told herself.

A studio monitor had shown how well the stage-lights sparkled on her sleeveless pink and silver dress. The design was perfect for her, giving her a long, elegant line. She had chosen well. *Britain should be proud of me tonight,* she thought. But it wouldn't be, of course. Yes, she knew a few close friends and family would cheer themselves hoarse in support, and she focused on them. But everyone else? She tried to blot out all the hateful, sneering faces she now saw all the time in England. The ones who had looked down on her at Heathrow on her way out to America last week. The ones who had snubbed her ever since the mighty Sir Paul McCartney had decreed he would divorce her. Since then Heather Mills had been dumped by the whole United Kingdom. She had flown to America to prove who she really was. To show how strong she could be and how much good she could do. But would America reject her too?

No self-pity, girl, she told herself. Her own terrible childhood had taught her to be strong. It had taught her to carry on, whatever life threw at her. And over the past month she had taken more blows than ever. The moment she had split from Sir Paul, a lifetime of hands-on charity work had been forgotten. The tens of thousands of amputees she had helped get new limbs were ignored. The endless war-torn roads and fields she had helped clear of landmines were dismissed. The campaigns she had launched to protect animal rights were derided. Instead the public were shown a new Heather Mills. An ugly one.

"Heather the £5,000 Hooker" and "Bisexual Heather sold body to Arabs for years" were the worst of the tabloid headlines all winter. "Go back to your bloody minefields, preferably without a metal detector," wrote one of her new critics on an internet forum. Suddenly everyone had taken sides against the girl who had spent a lifetime trying to do good. Her friends said she was a saint. The rest of the world suddenly screamed that she was a sinner. Heather said she was a victim. The public said she was a liar, a cheat and worse. All she had ever wanted was to be loved. Now she looked set to be shunned. Her whole crazy life suddenly seemed more upside down than ever.

Worst of all, whenever Heather thought things had hit rock bottom, she found there was always further to fall—as she would admit in a series of sensational television interviews the following year. In London, on the final day of October 2007, she would speak of death threats, of being close to suicide and of getting worse press than pedophiles. Her face deathly pale, she compared herself to the late Princess Diana and said the paparazzi—and other mysterious figures—were putting her life in near constant danger.

"Do you fear for your life?" she was asked by a stunned reporter from the BBC. "Yes, I do. Yes, I do," Heather replied, close to tears. More extraordinary still, she spoke of "a box of evidence that's going to a certain person should anything happen to [her]." It was explosive, headline-grabbing stuff from a woman clearly on the edge.

And it seemed there was much more to come. Heather then spoke to NBC's *Today* show and to a host of reporters on both sides of the Atlantic. She said Sir Paul's daughter Stella had been jealous of her marriage from the start—and had done everything in her power to destroy it. Then, Heather dropped her next bombshell.

Heather said she had recorded hours of conversations with Sir Paul as their marriage had imploded. The pair had apparently discussed their sex life at length—and Heather hinted at allegations of domestic violence in Paul's marriage to Linda. But what would worry the former Beatle the most was Heather's threat. She said she was prepared to go public with the tapes once their divorce settlement was agreed. Whatever Paul might have hoped, Heather certainly wasn't going to go quietly.

But in 2006, on the sound stage in Los Angeles, all this horror was still to come.

Today you've got a job to do, Heather. Today it's time to dance, she told herself. Then, finally, she got her chance. The *Dancing with the Stars* orchestra began to play and Heather's fears disappeared, just as she knew they would. Arching her back, she flung up her arms, shook her hips and shimmied across the stage towards Jonathan. Her dress caught even more of the studio lights. She was smiling broadly and she had a very sexy secret in her mind. Millions of dance fans were about to get an eye-popping surprise.

Dance your way out of all of this, Heather.

Still swaying to the rhythms, Heather tossed back her hair and stopped at the edge of the upper platform. Jonathan remained still and kept his eyes down as Heather put her hands on his shoulders. Then she did it. Slipping her fingers inside his elegant, gray waistcoat, she suddenly ripped it wide open. Jonathan's bare chest was fully exposed. The audience gasped— then cheered. Jonathan's skin was as smooth as a baby's. He and Heather had painstakingly waxed it bare the night before. It was pure dance theater. It was a triumph. Smiling as the applause got louder, Heather looked over at the three laughing judges.

And she winked.

She swept down final three steps onto the studio's main stage. She said a silent prayer of thanks as she made it—there were no steps in her rehearsal studio so tackling these in high heels was always going to be a tough test. Any dancer might have tripped at this point. Heather, with her false left leg, was at more risk than most. But she passed the test. Now on solid ground, she threw inhibition aside and exploded. The samba is the hottest, sexiest dance around. She didn't plan to disappoint. Hadn't she come to America to enjoy and redeem herself, she asked. Tonight she would prove it. She would dance the samba as if her life depended on it.

And, funnily enough…it really did.

As the music rang out, she and Jonathan paced, shimmied and strutted their way across the full length of the stage. There were deep dips, wild arm gestures, wide swings and wonderful stretches. One moment the pair was standing side by side, shaking their bodies down to the studio floor in total harmony, and the next, they were on their feet and in each other's arms. That night in particular the audience seemed to love it. There was applause as the pair approached their crescendo with four big switches and two huge smiles.

Then it happened.

Jonathan dipped to his knees and turned to face his partner. Heather looked directly into his eyes. She swung her hips as she strode up to him. Then she stopped, lifted her right leg on to his left shoulder for their final triumphant set-piece pose. All of her weight was supported on her artificial leg. She thrust up her arms, twisted her upper body to face the cameras. And then she fell.

She and Jonathan were exactly one minute and forty-five seconds into their one minute fifty second routine. They had so nearly nailed it. But as the audience rose up from their seats in shock, Heather was suddenly falling backwards, sliding across the studio floor where she landed in an embarrassed, undignified heap. For a split second, no one moved. Jonathan was first to recover. He reached over, desperate to get to his partner and help her back onto her feet. But Heather was ahead of him. She gave an all but imperceptible shake of her head and mouthed the word "no." Almost in the same moment that she had fallen, Heather had already started to stand up again. She had spent a lifetime being knocked to the ground. She had spent a lifetime picking herself up from the floor and carrying on regardless.

There was no way on earth she was going to stop now.

CHAPTER ONE

The First Tragedy

Heather was six years old when the two police officers knocked on her family's front door. She let them in and couldn't stop staring at their uniforms. They looked as if they had walked off a television cop show. Both of them were smiling, but Heather didn't smile back. Even at six, she knew it was never good news when the police turned up unexpectedly late at night.

The police found Heather's brother, Shane, watching television while her young sister, Fiona, was asleep on the sofa. It was 1974, their parents were on a rare night out and a neighbor had come 'round to look after them for the evening. Everyone had been having a fun night. The children were staying up a lot later than normal and were thrilled to be breaking some of the family's strict house rules. But then the female police officer knelt down next to the three children on the sofa. In her softest voice, she told them that they would have to listen carefully and be very brave. Their mummy and daddy had been in a car accident. They were in the hospital. It was serious.

Today, the rest of that awful night is just a blur. But Heather remembers that their babysitter's mother rushed into the house to take charge of the situation. She remembers being told it could be days before she would be able to visit her mum and dad in hospital. Most of all, she remembers hearing the policeman say her mum had nearly lost her leg. Less than three hours earlier, Beatrice Mills had been making her children laugh by dancing around the house as she prepared for her big night out. Now it seemed as if she might never walk again.

It would be six long months before Heather's mother was discharged from Newcastle General Hospital. By then, almost every part of Heather's life had changed. Her childhood had effectively ended, almost before it had begun. The day after the accident, Heather's grandmother rushed 400 miles from England's south coast to look after the children. She cared for them for a week and Heather wanted her to stay forever. She felt safe when her grandmother was around. But, after seven days, her dad Mark was released from hospital after being treated for minor head injuries, mild concussion, cuts and bruises. He was going to be back in charge at home. Heather knew, at six years old, that this meant trouble.

For three nights, she heard her dad and grandmother have fierce fights about the cause of the car accident and his behavior immediately afterwards. Heather listened in on the fights with tears in her eyes. She couldn't believe what she was hearing about her dad. It seemed that her mother had been thrown out of the car when it had hit a truck at a blind corner that awful night. As her mother lay crying on the edge of the road, Beatrice had felt the blood pour out of her near severed left leg. If she moved at all, she feared she might lose the limb completely. But she said that instead of offering her comfort, her husband's first act had been to pull her new fur coat from under her. He wanted to make sure it wasn't damaged by his wife's blood. Heather heard her grandmother say she could never forgive her son for acting so callously. So as soon as his bandages were removed, she walked out. She left his house and left him in sole charge of caring for Heather, Fiona and Shane.

Unfortunately, Mark Mills wasn't equipped to care for anyone. He was volatile, angry and the ultimate male chauvinist. He had always expected his wife to shop, cook and clean for him. With his wife in the hospital, he simply expected his children to step in and take over. And as they struggled to cope, he was planning another surprise. Driving home from one of their first hospital visits, he told them they had to pack their bags. They were leaving the wonderful house in the country where their memories of their mother were strongest. They were moving on to a coastal Navy base ten miles north of Newcastle so he could start a new job in the detention center.

"What about Ben?" Heather asked nervously. Her pet dog had slept on her bed every night since the accident and she couldn't bear to go anywhere without him.

"We'll have to give him away," she was told curtly. Dogs weren't allowed on the naval base. The subject was not up for discussion. Their pet cat, Tigga, and the goat the family had adopted from the nearby farm would also have to be left behind. The three children, nine-year-old Shane, six-year-old Heather and four-year-old Fiona were going to be on their own.

Living on a Naval base was an incredibly isolating experience for the children. They were cut off from the world by barbed wire fences and watchtowers. The huge packs of noisy, uniformed cadets made Heather nervous and their new home felt alien and uncomfortable. She was also on tenterhooks waiting for her father to explode in anger over something utterly trivial. That was how he was. That was why the Mills children were always so nervous. But after just a couple of tense and unhappy weeks on the Naval base, Heather was moved away.

Mark decided he couldn't cope with three young children in his house. He was happy to carry on looking after his son, Shane. But he wanted Heather and Fiona to be taken into foster care and looked after somewhere else. It was Heather's first big rejection.

Looking back, Heather says she's not sure what made her cry the most the day she and her sister packed their bags. Was it saying goodbye to their tearful, lost-looking brother? Or was it facing the unknown of life in a children's home? She missed her mother so much. When Beatrice had been around, life had been warm and happy. Now every day felt cold and frightening.

Fortunately, Heather and Fiona got lucky. They were moved to a children's center on the edge of Newcastle set amidst plenty of open fields. The staff members were kind, the girls made friends, and they were thrilled to finally have proper meals served three times a day. But for all this, what Heather wanted most was her mother. She wanted her family to get back together again. She would soon learn to be wary of what she wished for.

Once a week for six months, her dad would drive to the children's home. He would have Shane with him and they all went to visit their mother in the hospital. They weren't good days. Sometimes, it seemed as if Beatrice would never be well enough to come home and play happy family. Heather remembers how much weight her mother had lost, how pale and tired she always looked. The children certainly weren't shielded from what had happened to their mother.

The surgeons had managed to save her leg, but only by putting steel pins and a metal plate below her knee. They had now begun a series of skin grafts to try and repair the external damage. It was gruesome stuff and their mother's leg often looked like something out of a horror film. But as the weeks went by, Heather learned to cope with the wounds. She also started to feel comfortable in the cold, clinical hospital wards.

The nurses encouraged her to help clean her mother's bandages. They explained what they were doing to try and stop the wounds from getting infected. Heather loved listening to the doctors and the surgeons as they used long words to explain exactly what might happen next. Most of all she loved the calm, professional way these adults spoke and acted. She was inspired by people who put others before themselves. For a while, she thought she, too, would like to be a nurse when she grew up. Then she did what would become a character trait: she set her sights higher. She decided she wanted to become a plastic surgeon.

In 1975, after six months of hospital visits, Heather and Fiona began what they hoped would be their last week in the children's home. Their mother had finally been released from the hospital. But was she strong enough to look after her family? Beatrice told her daughters that she needed a few days to see if she could really cope on her crutches. Heather was beside herself with nerves as she waited to hear from her mom. She couldn't bear a second rejection. She wasn't old enough to understand why her mother might not be able to care for her.

Fortunately, Beatrice did decide to put her family first. She tried desperately to run the ugly Naval house while she recuperated from her injuries. She also tried to shield her children from their increasingly volatile father. Heather says that the anger inside her father seemed to have intensified since the accident. She watched as he began checking up on his injured wife's housework. She saw him lashing out if he thought Beatrice hadn't dusted every surface or vacuumed every inch of the carpeted-floor. He started to complain about her cooking and her appearance. The late night arguments that Heather remembered from their old house began with even more regularity.

"Sticks and stones can break my bones, but words can never hurt me." The phrase helped all three of the Mills children through those endless disputes. They hated the shouts and the screams. But they knew that unless their dad became violent they would all be able to cope. It was then that Mark became violent. Heather remembers him kicking her mother's crutches away after one fight. She heard that he had punched one of the naval cadets in the face after another.

That second incident had the biggest repercussions. Mark lost his job and the family had to leave the base. They moved to a small town on the coast, Heather's fourth home in three years. But money problems meant they were there for less than three months when their bags had to be packed yet again. This time the family was heading down-market. Detached houses with nice gardens were in their past. Their new home was a tiny apartment in a big social housing development. It was as ugly as hell.

Waterloo Court was in Washington, a decaying mining settlement 10 miles south of Newcastle. Heather remembers the graffiti, the vandalized stairwells, the stench of urine in all the public areas. Their neighbors seemed to argue as often as her own parents and at night Heather remembers the sound of kids running wild, of breaking glass and barking dogs. The walls of her new bedroom seemed to be crowding in on her. She simply couldn't imagine how her life could possibly get any worse.

"Would you like to buy a tapestry for ten pence?"

When Heather had been in the children's home with Fiona, they had each been given twenty-five pence a week in pocket money. When they moved out, they got nothing. So Heather decided to try and earn herself an income. She was seven years old. She spent weeks trying to work out what people at Waterloo Court might pay for doing odd jobs. No one was interested and most of the neighbors seemed to let their dogs run wild rather than needing anyone to walk them. In the end, she decided to try and make things. Her teachers had praised the mini-tapestries she had produced in a craft lesson so she spent night after night stockpiling a whole set of them in her bedroom. She decided to go knocking on doors to try and sell them.

A middle-aged man answered one of the first doors Heather tried. He looked at her and smiled. He asked if she wanted to come inside and she said yes. The door behind her closed. Inside the flat, the man sat down next to her and praised her work. He paid for every single one of her tapestries. Then he asked if she liked playing sports. Warning bells would have rung for any adult, or for many older children, but for Heather they remained silent. She said she enjoyed swimming and the man said he was a swimming coach. A terrible part of Heather's future was sealed.

Heather agreed to join the man's private swimming club and he was clever. Not only did he agree that she should ask her parents' permission before the first session, he said he would come 'round personally to reassure them that all was well. When he turned up, he got lucky.

Heather's mother had always been keen to get her children interested in sports. Before the car accident she had been a great tennis player as well as a dancer. She had always hoped her children would share the same love of exercise. She hated that she could no longer teach them sports herself. The offer of swimming lessons from this man they would only know as "Mr. Morris" was like an answer to a prayer.

So Heather headed off on a set of weekly swimming lessons. Her strokes improved dramatically. She was growing taller all the time and had an impressive reach for her age. She was also determined. If a girl in her class could do five lengths, then Heather had to do ten. If an older girl could cover a certain distance in twenty-five minutes, then Heather had to cover it in twenty. Heather Mills had already decided that she would never be beaten. So did it matter if her new instructor would sometimes climb into the pool to swim alongside her during one of the private classes? Did it matter if he held her body up in the water so she could learn a more streamlined swimming position? Was it a problem that he would reach his arms around her body to show her just how to pull on the water?

The exact details of what happened next have been lost in time. What is known is that Heather and one of her neighbors were both entered in a three-day swimming competition some 30 miles away in the northern town of Darlington. Heather was a few years younger than her neighbor, Margaret, but she was convinced she could beat her in a proper race. She couldn't understand why Margaret seemed so unwilling to make the trip.

The girls never made it to Darlington. Their instructor called them into his flat just before they had been due to leave. He said he needed to find some missing paperwork. Then he locked the door and kept them there for the full three days they were supposed to be at the competition.

Heather says the man never did more than "fondle" her while she was kept a prisoner. But she heard Margaret cry when she was taken into his bedroom. And she was told she would be killed if she tried to escape. On the third day, Margaret did manage to leave the flat. Just after their captor left to try and find her, the police broke down the door and took a screaming, crying Heather back to her parents. Tragically, her ordeal was far from over. After coaxing a statement out of her, the police decided they needed to do a full medical examination. Heather and her mother went to the police station in Sunderland. Heather remembers the chilling, clinical nature of the exam. She remembers the single piece of candy she was given when it was over.

What we now know is that the pedophile swimming teacher went on the run and killed himself by jumping off a cliff overlooking the North Sea. That is how the story should have ended for Heather. But her personal nightmare had several more years to run. For three years, no one told her that her captor was dead. The idea had been to spare her feelings. The result was that she spent three years watching out for the man at every street corner. Between the ages of seven and ten, she spent every day trying to prepare herself to give evidence against him in court. For three terrible years she was terrified that he might come 'round to kill her to try and stop the case.

Another year, another new home. To this day, Heather says she has never found out exactly what her dad did to earn his money after they left the Naval base. But after a year in their ugly social housing, the cash certainly seemed to be coming in again. In 1976, the family moved a few miles from the derelict center of Washington to a leafier suburb and a detached, single-story home.

Mark took up photography and bought a lot of expensive equipment. Beatrice decided to go back to college. She enrolled at Newcastle University to study psychology and Heather saw some slow, but wonderful changes. Bit by bit, the confident, well-groomed woman Heather remembered from yesteryear seemed to be coming back. Beatrice started wearing makeup again. She bought new clothes. She was walking without her crutches or even a stick. Without saying a word, Beatrice told her eldest daughter that you can bounce back from tragedy.

She taught her that you can reinvent yourself and should never give up on your dreams.

Out of nowhere Heather also remembers her dad developing a passion for theater, dance and opera. He joined a circuit of small business owners and self-employed people who all helped each other up the financial ladder. She didn't know it at the time, but as she helped out at some of the social functions and sat at the back of so many of the meetings, Heather was learning how to network. Her father could hardly have been a better teacher. Outsiders only ever saw his charm. They believed his promises and were carried away by his sudden enthusiasm for the arts. He ended up as chairman of Newcastle Theater Royal, helping with all the rehearsals, watching every performance and mingling with all the stars.

Because Mark needed to be at the theater most evenings, the family managed to settle down to a comfortable routine without him. Gone were the vicious squabbles over dinner. The rejected food, broken plates, and smashed windows were forgotten. The early evening arguments over the cleaning and the demands that the children finish off the jobs he said their mother had missed were just memories. Heather dared to hope that she might be able to put down some roots. She wanted to stay in a single school for more than a year. She wanted to be able to do her homework in peace. She wanted to watch her beautiful mother blossom again as her accident became a distant memory.

Once more she was about to be very badly disappointed.

It had begun like any other day. Heather was nine, Shane was twelve and Fiona was seven. They had breakfast with their mum, packed their bags for school and headed off as usual. But at the end of the day they came home to an empty house.

"What are we going to eat?" Fiona asked. She and Heather looked around to see if their mother had left anything to be heated up later, but there was nothing. There was no note, either, even though their mum always left one if she was going to be home late. Puzzled, they all carried on with their usual routine as much as possible. Shane started his homework and Heather and Fiona raided the fridge in case dinner was going to be particularly late.

Then it happened.

The front door slammed open, but it was their dad, not their mum who raced through it. His face was hard and cold and Heather remembers standing in front of him in the family room. She was desperately trying to work out if she had inadvertently done something to annoy him. And where was their mother? As usual, the memories of that terrible night just three years earlier came flooding back. Had history repeated itself? Would their dad be the one to give them the bad news this time, instead of a kindly police officer? Heather felt herself shiver as she waited for her dad to speak.

When he did she almost stopped breathing with shock. There had been no accident, but her mother wasn't coming back.

"She has met another man," they were told. "She's left us."

It would be nearly two years before Heather saw or heard from her mother again.

CHAPTER TWO

All Alone

Morning after morning Heather jumped out of bed to see if her mother had written to her. No letters ever came. She, Fiona and Shane had endless discussions about what might have happened. They constantly tried to pluck up the courage to ask their dad for more information. But they were all too scared. They had seen him lash out at their mother and at everyone else too many times. None of them wanted to feel his fists as well. So, where was their mother?

Even at nine years old, Heather felt too embarrassed to ask the teachers or her friends at school. They might know the truth, but Heather didn't want to admit that her mother didn't love her. She was too ashamed to tell her neighbors she had been abandoned. Instead, she pretended that she knew everything that had been going on and was entirely happy with it. Heather discovered that she was surprisingly good at covering up and telling lies.

Behind closed doors, the happy home that had built up over the past year had been shattered. With three young children to supposedly care for, Mark was unable to spend every evening at his beloved theater. So he stayed home every night—and took out his frustration on his kids. There was no question that they would all have to step in once more to do the work their dad associated with women. Mark expected his house to be cleaned just as well as it had been in the past. But just as the three children built up a routine to get the job done, they were disrupted yet again. The wonderful income he had been earning seemed to have dried up. Once more they could no longer afford to stay in their house. Once more the bags were packed and they moved to a different rented home in a different suburb. For Heather, this latest move was the worst of all. What if her mother didn't know their new address? What would happen to her letters, if she ever decided to write?

Heather felt overwhelmingly lonely in their new home. She felt isolated from her old friends, totally cut off even from the memory of her mother. But she had no time to grieve. Her dad had put a cleaning schedule on their new kitchen wall. Each of his children had specific tasks to complete every day. Heather had an extra challenge. She was to be in charge of the family's increasingly erratic food budget. She would shop and help cook every day. She was nine years old.

Years later, what angers Heather is the fact that no adults ever intervened in her increasingly dysfunctional family. "I was slipping behind at school because I was so tired and had so much to do at home. But no one thought to ask why. No one asked why I wasn't doing my homework or why I fell asleep in class," she says.

None of the shopkeepers seemed to ask why it was a nine-year-old girl who would always be buying food, especially as she was so clearly choosing the items herself rather than checking them off a list provided by her parents. The shopping sessions were tough. Heather often had no more than the equivalent of two dollars a day. She was forced to go from shop to shop trying to find cheap food. She traded down from chicken to rabbit. When even rabbit was out of her reach, she used canned beans instead of meat in casseroles. For school lunches, she made jelly sandwiches and wove wonderful stories for Fiona and Shane so they could all imagine they were eating turkey with cranberry sauce and stuffing.

The feminist writer Germaine Greer is one of many commentators who agree all this would have a profound effect on Heather for the rest of her life. "Heather, who needed mothering as much as any child, had to play the role of parent," says Greer. She added that Heather's position in the family group brought other complications. "Heather was a big sister, and big sisters are often not very good at attending to their own needs, or at understanding their own feelings. Especially when they grew up protecting and providing for younger siblings who they perceived to be in greater need than themselves." Heather's mother, who unknown to her daughter was continuing to take psychology classes in London, might have agreed. Others said Heather had suffered a textbook case of what is known as: "sequential abandonment and inappropriate responsibility." It would cast a very long shadow in the years ahead.

By the time Heather was ten, she had started stealing the food she couldn't afford to buy.

She admits she was good at it. A can here, a couple of vegetables there, a packet of pasta when she thought no one was looking. Most of the time she got away with it. The first time she was caught, she got a warning. The next time, the store manager said he would report her to the police. Still no one bothered to ask why such a young girl would need to steal food. The family continued to fall through the net that was supposed to protect them. Heather learned habits she would take years to break. When she wasn't stealing groceries, she was lying to officials about their father. She was the one he made answer the door when the council came round to ask about their unpaid rent. She had to say he was out and pass on messages she knew he would ignore. For years she lived in fear that they would be forced to leave yet another house and start afresh in yet another school.

As her twelfth birthday approached, Heather was in danger of losing her way for good. She was paying less and less attention in school and had fallen in with a bad set of pupils. She loved sports, but hated classrooms. She needed a wake-up call.

That moment came on a week-long field trip to the mountains of Wales. Heather was thrilled to be away from the responsibilities of home, though she remembers worrying endlessly about how her younger sister would cope without her. She loved the intensity of the exercise the class was forced to do and she wanted to lead the hikes, the hill-climbs and the orienteering expeditions. Everything about the field trip seemed to remind her of happier times. She remembered family holidays to Wales as a little girl. Even the goat that she befriended near her dormitory reminded her of the pets she had cared for before her mother's accident. It was when she was petting the little goat one morning that she turned round and got the shock of her life. Her mother was walking down the path towards her. And she looked fantastic.

As mother and daughter hugged and cried, Heather realized that they weren't alone. A tall, distinguished-looking man was standing watching them from a distance. Heather instinctively knew who he was. He must be her mother's new man, she thought through her tears. He must be the reason she left us. She hated him on sight.

"Heather, I want you to meet someone very special."

Hardly able to see through her tears, Heather couldn't believe she was being forced to say hello to the man who had ruined her life. And as she looked up at him she suddenly realized that she had seen him before. He had dropped their mother off at home one afternoon, years ago. Beatrice had told the children he was at university with her, but the neighbors had said he was actually a famous actor who had been appearing in a play at the theater in Newcastle. Suddenly lots of pieces started to fall into place.

"This is Charles," Heather was told and she shook hands with him, her heart pounding.

Her mother said she had spoken to the teachers and had permission to take Heather out for lunch. Heather didn't care where they went or what they did. She turned her back on Charles. She just wanted to hold on to her mother. She didn't want her to ever leave again. As the three of them sat in the sunshine outside a country pub, Heather found out exactly what had been happening for the past 18 months. Her mother had written to her, almost every week. But her dad must have thrown the letters away. Beatrice and Charles had a small flat in London and Beatrice was working in a hospice there. She said she tried to help people find peace before they died. Charles, meanwhile, was acting in a play in London called *The Mousetrap*. It all sounded incredibly grown-up and exciting. Heather could see why her mother had gone. On the drive back to the children's center, Heather begged her mum to keep on writing. She vowed she would be brave enough to challenge her dad about the letters.

"Can I come and visit you in London?" she asked, hardly daring to ask in case she got another rejection. But her mother said she could. They agreed that Heather would take the bus down at the start of the summer holidays, in less than two months' time. Then it was goodbye.

"I'm very sorry I had to leave, Heather."

Just eight words. It wasn't a proper apology and it didn't even come close to being a proper explanation of what she had done. But it was enough for Heather. At last she knew she hadn't driven her mother away. It hadn't been her fault and she could finally stop feeling guilty.

For the rest of the school term, Heather's teachers noticed a big change in her. She was paying more attention in class. She was trying harder and misbehaving less. Now her mother was back in her life and Heather desperately wanted to make her proud. She started doing her homework properly and slowly edged away from some of the troublemakers in the school yard. And she counted the days until the summer holiday when she could see her mother again.

The bus ride from Newcastle Central Station to London's Victoria Bus Station takes nearly eight hours and involves more than a dozen stops. Not many twelve-year-old girls do the journey on their own, but Heather was fearless. Yes, she had moments of awful doubt when she imagined arriving in the big city to find her mother wasn't there. And yes, she knew that her mother's track record meant that this was a very real possibility. But she had to carry on. She wanted to see her more than anything. Fortunately, Beatrice was waiting for the bus as promised. They hugged, they laughed and walked hand in hand to the subway station. Heather had her first trip on the London Underground as they headed south of the River Thames to Clapham. Immediately after that, the bubble burst.

Her mother's home was worse than anywhere the family had ever lived up in Newcastle. Worse even than the smallest of flats in Waterloo Court. Beatrice and Charles had a single room in a noisy shared building. There was a bed, a closet, a tiny sink and an ancient stove along one wall, nothing else. The building was old and dark and everything smelled of decay and despair. Heather was going to sleep in an even smaller, darker room across the communal hall. The door had a big lock on it and Heather nearly started to cry as she put her little bag on the sagging bed and tried to pretend everything was OK. No wonder her mum had said she had to come on her own. No wonder Fiona and Shane had to make separate trips later in the summer.

Beatrice rushed her daughter out of the tiny room and off to one of Clapham's parks to try and cheer her up. They then took in some of the big tourist sights. As they walked, Heather remembers spotting a big difference between London and Washington. At home in Washington, everyone seemed to be poor so nobody seemed to care. But wherever she went in London, Heather realized she always saw at least one person who looked rich. And even at twelve, Heather knew that the rich were different. She saw a kind of confidence in their eyes, a confidence she had never felt herself. Years later she says she learned one simple fact on that first trip to London. It was that money gives you power. If she had money, she was convinced everything in her life would come together. Her mother would love her and her father would treat her better. Money, she felt, could change everything.

Having waited so long to spend a week with her mother in London, Heather couldn't believe that she was soon desperate to go back home. She loved being with her mother and rushed to help her with her makeup every morning. But it was hard to relax. Charles was always sleeping on the other half of the bed as they sat in front of the mirror. When he was awake, Heather always felt in the way. She hated having to share her mother's attention with him because she already knew that he would always come first. This realization took all the optimism out of Heather's soul. Back in Newcastle, she joined a new school and began to drift back towards the troublemakers. She stopped paying attention in class and no longer cared about her homework. Making her mother proud didn't seem very important any more. She wasn't sure Beatrice would even notice. To make matters worse, Heather was also facing new pressures at home. Her dad was no longer content to have his children running his house. Now he wanted them to help run his business as well.

After leaving the theater, Mark had become obsessed with opera—Wagner's operas in particular. He believed he could put together a unique theatrical presentation of the *Ring Cycle*. He thought it was going to make his fortune. The presentation involved projecting thousands of slides on big screens while the music played. It sounds small-scale today, but in the early 1980s, Mark reckoned it was on the cutting edge of cool. Problem was, he couldn't do it all on his own.

Every night Heather, Fiona and Shane had to cut pictures out of books and magazines for their dad to photograph. When the negatives came back they had to mount them onto home-made slides. It was laborious, meticulous work that kept the children up past midnight almost every night. And, as usual, Mark expected perfection. But if Heather thought the pressure was on when they helped put together the slides, it was nothing compared to the performances themselves. After some try-outs in and around Newcastle, Mark managed to get big bookings— including at the Edinburgh Festival and the Queen Elizabeth Hall in London. When the time came, Mark excelled at greeting the audiences and controlling the music. But behind the scenes, he left his children to work nearly a dozen manual slide projectors at a time. It was tense, exhausting stuff. But like every other get-rich-quick scheme Mark had ever had, it would soon end in tears. First, he was called in by his children's headmaster, who was unhappy about the number of days off his children took while his show was on the road. Then, at a big London show, the rented equipment broke down and the audience had to have its money refunded. In public, Mark displayed his usual bravado, claiming he was happy to move on to other areas and focus on a new youth training scheme he had come up with for musicians. In private, his anger grew.

"He treated us like slaves. He was a bully and a coward," Fiona says of her dad during this period. The only thing that made life easier for the children was that he started disappearing for days and then weeks at a time. He said he was working with disadvantaged children and reports of his charity work even made the local papers. Why this charity never began at home was never explained to them.

By the time Heather became a teenager, she was more than ready to rebel. Her closest friend was Julia Quinn, a neighbor a couple of years older than her. She lived in the kind of happy home the Mills children had only ever read about. Julia wanted to take Heather to her first disco in a nearby community center. It was an alcohol-free Thursday night party and Heather was desperate to go because she loved to dance. She knew she was fit enough to stay on the floor all night. But something was worrying her: boys.

Heather had grown up fast. She was taller than almost everyone else in her class and had been among the first to need a bra. The boys in the years above had started to notice her fast-developing figure. But they didn't come too close. Heather remembers having bad skin and buck teeth. She had already developed a desperate fear of rejection. The idea of being left a wallflower in a suburban disco filled her with horror.

She and Julia spent hours trying different types of make-up to hide her acne. In her strong moments, Heather was convinced she could hide her blemishes and pass for fifteen or even older. But in her weak moments, she was terrified of being dumped on the dance floor. She needed courage and she found it in stolen alcohol.

The shoplifting skills that had helped her stretch the family's housekeeping money in the bad times were now good enough to smuggle big bottles of hard cider out of local supermarkets. Heather and Julia would drink them inside a derelict shop they had broken into near the town center. Sometimes they would mix the cider with beer to get an even bigger kick. Heather forgot all about her bad skin and Bugs Bunny teeth. She danced until the lights went up. She even flirted with the boys. It turned out she was pretty good at it.

The early 1980s were not the best of times to be in the North East of England. Today, Newcastle City Center is booming. It has a chic waterside quarter, a world-class concert hall in the Sage and an endless number of bars, clubs and restaurants. The local economy has created thousands of new jobs and young people who left the area a decade ago are moving back to ride this prosperous new wave.

When fifteen-year-old Heather started to sit through career counseling in school, the prospects were completely different. All people talked about was unemployment. Even the teachers focused on what pupils couldn't do or shouldn't try. Most of the pupils at her school moved from pointless training schemes to welfare benefits. Being a teenage mother still seemed a viable career option. Petty crime was the most obvious way to get rich. Heather had long since forgotten her dreams of becoming a nurse or plastic surgeon. Sometimes when she went down to London to visit her mother she was briefly inspired by the thought of being a counsellor. But no one told her how to pursue the option. She was also starting to feel like a fish out of water wherever she was. London seemed exciting and she wanted to be there with her mother. But she didn't want to be there with Charles. Her hometown was great because she liked the discos and had so many good friends. But she didn't want to be there with her father.

She started to dream about leaving home. Things had started to go wrong with her dad's youth training scheme, and the bailiffs were back at the door all the time trying to take away all the goods he had bought on credit. All she wanted was a bit of stability. But she wasn't going to get it. It seemed that the Mills family had yet another surprise to spring.

"Heather's in trouble!"

"Heather's going to get the cane."

"Heather's going to be expelled!"

All of the kids in Heather's class started snickering when the announcement came over the public address system. She had been called her to the headmaster's office in the middle of afternoon lessons. Heather tried to swagger out of the class as if she didn't care. But her mind was racing. What had she done? She had never even met the headmaster, let alone been called to his study. How bad could this be? As she walked down the corridor to the staff rooms, another announcement rang out. Fiona was being called to the headmaster's office as well. Then, there was another announcement. This time they wanted Shane. Heather started to walk faster. This was bad.

When she arrived, she froze. Fiona and Shane had managed to get there first and they weren't alone. Two uniformed police officers were standing by the headmaster's desk. One of them was a woman. Heather was transported right back to the evening her mother had nearly lost her leg. Could she have been in another accident? Was she dead? Heather felt her breathing quicken. She leaned on the door frame because she knew she had to stay strong. The policeman spoke first. It turned out to have nothing to do with Beatrice. The man had just come from the local court. Their father had been sent to prison.

CHAPTER THREE

The Streets of London

Heather, Fiona and Shane sat in silence as they were driven to a neighbor's house in a police car. Their mother was coming up from London and their grandmother was on her way from the south coast. The three children had no idea what was going to happen to them. It was dark when Beatrice arrived and she sent the children straight to bed.

"We'll decide what we are all going to do in the morning," she said. Heather couldn't look at her. She was furious that Charles had travelled north alongside her. She had hoped she might for once have had her mother to herself. "We think it would be best if Shane goes to live with Grandma in Brighton and you and Fiona come back to London with Charles and me." Their mother dropped the bombshell over breakfast the next day. The tears began straight away. However bad things had been in their childhood, the three of them had always known they could rely on each other. They had only survived by being strong together. They couldn't imagine being split up.

"Can't we just stay here? We're old enough," they begged. They'd certainly looked after themselves without adult supervision for long enough in the past. But their mother and their grandmother had made up their minds. Heather, catching Charles's eye, wasn't sure about his. She decided he was probably the one person in the room who was more upset about the new arrangements than they were. Within a matter of hours, Heather's whole life was in a pair of black plastic bags. The doors to their old house were locked and she, Fiona and Shane climbed into the back of the big rented truck. They were leaving their home in Lambton, their friends and their school. Heather didn't go to say goodbye to any of the neighbors. She was too ashamed.

In London, she was spared the tiny room in her mother's first Clapham flat. Beatrice and Charles had moved into a new house. They now rented a couple of ground floor rooms in a bigger property owned by an elderly bachelor they had met at church. The landlord had agreed that Heather and Fiona could each have a bedroom up in his part of the property. Bearing in mind Heather's experiences with her swimming coach, she was understandably nervous. But Norman, her mother's landlord, was a true gentleman. The rooms he offered the girls were dark and old and depressing. But his welcome was warm. Charles was a different story. He had already raised a family of his own. He showed no signs of wanting to help raise anyone else's. He, Heather and Fiona edged around each other in the big, cold house. If he was in the one warm family room, they would head up to their chilly bedrooms. If they went in the kitchen, he would leave. They spoke as little as possible and it broke Heather's heart to see that her mother normally followed her partner rather than sticking with her girls. She shouldn't have been surprised. But it would always hurt.

The next problems came at school. Heather and Fiona were enrolled in Hydeburn School, the only school that would accept them halfway through the academic year. It was a big, rough South London high school in an area rife with gangs and drugs. Heather and Fiona could not have been more different than the tough, streetwise multi-ethnic London girls in their classes. They were both tall, blond and had harsh northern accents. "They were regularly bullied by the other girls because they stood out so much," remembers Charles, who occasionally drove the kids to school and tried to watch out for the girls when he wasn't working.

Heather and Fiona had other ideas about how to fit in. They dyed their hair and created matching punk-style cuts to show they weren't squares. They got into fights and won them to earn respect. They tried to tune in to the London accent so they could at least understand what everyone else was talking about. Unfortunately, Heather and Fiona's chances of making real friends at Hydeburn School were dashed when they were sent back up north for the whole of the summer holidays. Charles had been diagnosed with stomach cancer and Beatrice didn't think she could care for him and her girls at the same time. Once more, Heather noticed that when her mother needed to choose, her girls came second. Once more, it hurt.

Looking back, that's probably why Heather went wild when she came back to London for the start of the new term. She had wanted her mother to love her—and to show it. She had given her so many second chances, made so many excuses for her. But she had seen this beautiful, capable woman put a man ahead of everything else. And not even a good man. First, the husband who beat and abused her. Now, the actor who froze out his partner's children. Heather vowed that when she fell in love she would never lose her self-respect. She would never let a man walk all over her.

As the tension mounted at home, Heather started to dream of escape. She wanted a new set of friends and a whole new life. She also thought she knew where she might find it. A carnival had moved onto the park a few streets away from her home, and Heather was entranced by the characters who worked in it. They were travelling people who never put down roots and never stayed in one place for long. Heather knew how they felt. She loved seeing how hard they worked, but how much they supported each other. That reminded her of her life with Fiona and Shane. She knew she was going absolutely nowhere at school and she had no idea what to do with her life. She decided to join the fair.

"Are there any jobs? Anything at all?"

"How old are you, love?"

In her autobiography, *A Single Step*, Heather has said she

was just thirteen when she plucked up the courage to ask one of the women at the fair for work. Her sister has since confirmed that this was a mistake. She was fifteen. A little wiser and more experienced, perhaps. But, still, far too young to be given a job by strangers. That's exactly what happened, however. Heather was offered work and told she could stay in a tiny camper on the fairground if she wanted. She worked every day the fair was open—until midnight, seven days a week in the late summer— and the jobs never stopped. She took tea and meals around to all the other workers. She picked up the trash, she cleaned vomit off the rides and tidied up the toys at the shooting galleries and ball tosses. She loved it.

It was when she was living on the fairgrounds that Heather met her first real boyfriend. His name was Peter and he was one of the first people she ever spoke to on the site. They tried to end up working in the same areas most evenings so they could chat for a while after the crowds had left. Peter was in his twenties and all the women seemed to want to be with him. But he wanted to spend his time with Heather. The fair soon left Clapham Common and all the campers and rides were moved to new pitches in other parts of South London. They moved every few weeks—Heather was in her element. She and Peter had still never kissed, but she was sure it was only a matter of time. The two people Heather missed back then were her sister and Julia. She didn't have any other close female friends and she desperately wanted someone to share her hopes with. What she didn't know was that she would also need someone to cry with when tragedy struck.

The shock came when Heather was setting up the rides one morning. Peter wasn't with her so she went over to his camper to find him. He didn't answer the door but she thought she could see him through the window. When some of the other workers broke the door down, they told her he was dead. There was a hypodermic syringe in his arm. He had overdosed on heroin. His whole life had been wasted. Once more, Heather was alone. Once more, there was worse to come.

She knew her mother had told some lies to her old school to stop the authorities coming round to find her. But she was still too young to be working full-time on a fairground. Paul's fellow workers told her the police were coming with the ambulance crew. She should leave now and never come back. The problem was that Heather had nowhere to go. She was too proud to go back to live with her mother and Charles. She couldn't admit that she hadn't been able to cope on her own. So she packed the few things she owned into the same black plastic bags that had marked all the moves she had ever made. Just like leaving Lambton, she left the fairground without saying goodbye to a single soul.

She disappeared into the Underground at High Barnet tube station with no idea of where she was going. By the time night fell, she had still not made up her mind. She was in central London, she was exhausted, scared and vulnerable. But she wouldn't be beaten. Out of nowhere, she remembered someone had once talked about all the homeless who congregated under the arches of Waterloo Station. "It's like a whole secret city of people," he had said. "It's a whole hidden world that no one even knows exists." This sounded good enough to Heather. She headed south towards Waterloo.

Just how many nights Heather slept on the street in London is unclear. She has said she survived under the railway arches for four months. Others say it couldn't have been as much as half that long. Some claim she only spent a few nights there when neighbors and friends of her mother couldn't take her in. But the time she did spend in Waterloo would continue to form her. Some of the lessons she learned on those mean streets are clearly present in her personality today. Many of her toughest attitudes were formed among the homeless and hopeless of South London.

Heather's enduring contempt for people who peddle drugs is one of them. So soon after losing Peter she couldn't bear to see any used syringes in the streets. Whenever she did, she got flashbacks of the one sticking out of her dead friend's arm. She wondered if another good person might have died after shooting up. Heather also learned that if you look hard enough you can find goodness in the least promising of situations. The men and women under the railway arches never once judged her. Many tried to help her, suggesting she should forgive her mother and return to her home. Yes, there were fights and drunken arguments and endless angry scenes. But there was also extreme kindness. The best of her new comrades would often share what little food they had.

Her final lesson was that if you want to pick yourself up off the floor you need to do it on your own. She dodged fares on the London Underground and she took full advantage of the handouts from the soup kitchens around the capital. But something made her hold back from begging. She didn't feel she was entitled to ask other people for money. They did jobs and earned their cash. Why should she expect to be given any of it just because she wasn't working herself? In the years ahead, when her charity work reached some of the world's worst trouble spots, Heather would see that only tough love could help some causes. She inflicted tough love upon herself while sleeping on the streets of London. "As a child, I stole food and I stole clothes just to survive," she would admit to Larry King in America years later. "But as an adult, I couldn't sit begging like some people do." Her uniquely flexible moral compass was already being formed. It would spring plenty of surprises in the months ahead.

One of Heather's old neighbors took her in after seeing her loitering in the streets of London one afternoon. She was horrified that the teenager had been sleeping on the streets—everyone had been told she had gone back up to school in Newcastle. After a lot of persuading, Heather was finally ready to make peace with her mother and Fiona. Charles was in a touring show and was often away, so Heather started to spend more time with her family. She also got her first weekend job, in a local jeweler's shop. It didn't go well.

Heather has never revealed the identity of the shop's owner, referring to him only as a Mr. Penrose when she speaks of this shameful chapter in her life. His real name was Jim Guy and Heather abused his trust very badly. After a couple of months in the shop, Heather decided to steal from him. It began one lunch hour when she grabbed a handful of gold chains from the store cupboard and hid them in her bag. Back in her room at home she examined her haul. There were literally dozens of chains. They must have been worth hundreds of pounds and Heather started to feel nervous. Had she taken too much too soon? Two days later she headed across South London to another shopping area and another jewelry shop. Taking a deep breath, she went in, asked to see the manager and offered her gold chains for sale. Could it have been more obvious that the teenage girl had stolen them? Probably not. But the shopkeeper bought them anyway. For a thousand pounds.

The roll of £50 notes felt as if they were burning a hole in Heather's bag. If she had been paid a thousand pounds then the chains must have been worth far more. All she had wanted when she had first grabbed them was a little bit of extra cash. Suddenly things seemed to have gotten very serious. What had she done? The police had been called to the jeweler's to investigate the missing goods and Heather was terrified that they would come to her home and find the money. So she decided to spend it. She bought a motor scooter, new clothes, huge amounts of makeup and skin care products. She took Fiona and friends on days out and bought everyone meals in the evenings. She went to an expensive hair salon and found a health spa for beauty treatments. Everyone noticed how good she had started to look. Her bad skin had cleared and her new confidence had turned her into an eye-catching young woman.

"You should be a model," she was told at the hair salon. She laughed. But she couldn't stop thinking about it.

At the jewelry shop, Jim Guy was at his wits' end. "I wasn't insured and it nearly put me out of business," he says. As the police continued their investigation he carried on quizzing his full and part-time staff. He had his eye on two of his long-term employees and was convinced that they were the guilty parties. "I never, never, ever thought it was Heather," he said afterwards. But the police had tracked down the jeweler who had bought the stash of chains and they had a clear description of the pretty young girl who had sold them.

"Heather Mills, you're under arrest."

The police arrived at Heather's home in a dawn raid—a bit over-dramatic for a petty theft and a female, teenage suspect. But it got the message across. Heather was terrified as she was led out into a police car. To this day, she remembers her final shock of that morning. Her mother didn't come to the police station with .her. She simply stood aside as her daughter was taken away. For so long, Heather had wanted her mother to notice and be proud of her. Now she had ruined everything. And she had no one to blame but herself.

Perhaps surprisingly, it was Charles who would come to her rescue. After Heather had been kept in the station overnight, he found a lawyer who had her released. When her case finally came before the court, the lawyer said Heather had learned her lesson. He argued that her endlessly disrupted childhood provided mitigating circumstances. She was put on probation and told to report to a court official once a week for the rest of the year. When he spoke of the case years later, Charles showed some rare sympathy for Heather. He seemed to understand why she had taken the gold chains. He recognized the demons that would torment her for the rest of her life. "Her terrible childhood was no lie and was the root of all her problems," he said. "She lost her mother during her most vulnerable and formative years, which obviously had a terrible effect on her. I was so sorry for her when she first came to live with us as she seemed such a troubled, confused young woman. All she has ever wanted to do is make something of herself. To change the person she was and to escape her past."

Straight after the court case, Heather managed to find another equally short-lived job. This time she worked in a croissant shop in Central London and she says she left because she hated the garish pink uniform. Others joked that she had to go because she ate too much of the stock. The staff were allowed to eat whatever they wanted on their breaks. But Heather reckons the owner hadn't realized just how many calories she could put away without gaining weight. So for whatever reason, she soon moved on.

Jobless, rootless and practically friendless, she decided to go back north for a couple of weeks. Her dad was out of prison and had a new girlfriend who would soon give birth to Heather's step-sister Claire. Heather's old pal, Julia, was always saying the nightlife in Newcastle was getting better all the time. It was time to get a taste of it. With bleached blond hair, deep blue eyeshadow and a tiny black leather mini-skirt, Heather looked a true child of the eighties on those big northern nights out. She and the girls went on long pub crawls, always ending up in nightclub called Sirrocco.

"We all drank cherry brandy and cider," remembers one of the crowd. "It was called a Knicker Dropper."

It was at Sirrocco that Heather met her first proper boyfriend. His name was Stephen Leyton and it turned out he had been one of the boys she had stared at and dreamed about many years ago at the old community club discos in Lampton. Steve lived in a tiny flat in the town—which Heather moved into—and worked in a nearby factory. Heather fell head over heels in love with him—and she couldn't bear to tell him she was only up north for a short break. "I think I'm going to stay another week or so," she told her sister on the phone. But she decided that if she could get a decent job she might just stay forever. The problem was she couldn't find any job, let alone a good one. Washington was still one of the most economically depressed parts of the country. The few jobs that were available certainly weren't going to be offered to a teenage girl with precious few qualifications and a criminal record. Heather was stuck and she hated sitting around all day waiting for Steve to come home from work. He was an old-fashioned gentleman, but she didn't want him to have to pay all of her bills. She wanted money of her own. After three months, she realized the only place she could earn it was back in London.

"I'm only going for a while. I'll make some money then I'll be back." She looked into Steve's eyes, desperate to persuade him that she had no choice.

"You're trying to say we're finished. Is that it?"

"No, of course not." She promised that she would come back up every weekend if she could afford it. And he could come down to London whenever he wanted. She was convinced that their long-distance love affair could work.

Back in London, Heather's next challenge was to earn money. As usual, her choice was largely determined by her background. Her mum had hardly ever worked and she had never really known what her dad ever did for a living. No one in Washington had ever talked of careers or callings. She just knew that sometimes her dad got work that paid well, sometimes he had nothing but debts. She only knew jobs as short-term, feast or famine opportunities. Nothing mattered but the amount of cash you got at the end of them. In 1985, Heather was confused and aimless. She was also a tall pretty girl with a fit body and a fantastic figure. No wonder she ended up in Soho.

The sex trade and the strip clubs were impossible to ignore in the streets and alleyways around London's Old Compton Street. Women stood in doorways, enticing men into the basement rooms where over-priced, watered-down champagne would be served at tiny tables. Big men ensured the bills were paid at the end of the evening. Heather's first Soho job was in a typical strip joint. She wore her tightest tops, her shortest skirts and her heaviest makeup to serve the drinks while the other girls chatted to the customers. She earned some money in tips, but soon realized she was making nowhere near as much as the girls who did the talking and headed off with their clients at the end of the night. Heather was on the point of asking the manager if she could change roles when the police raided the bar and closed it down. But by now Heather knew how to make easy money. She wasn't going to give up.

Within a week, she was back behind another Soho bar, this time making cocktails and earning a slightly better basic wage. One of the other workers lived close to the club so Heather asked if she could move in with her to cut her commuting costs. She was about to enter a whole new world. Her new landlady was a part-time pin-up model called Gloria. She believed the teenage Heather was the perfect person to follow in her footsteps.

CHAPTER FOUR

In Front of the Cameras

The photography studio out in London's East End was cold and harshly lit. Heather stood in front of a white sheet wearing a swimsuit left behind by another model. The cameraman snapped away. Heather changed poses. She took off the swimsuit and put on a man's jacket, though the material barely stretched across her naked chest. "Get them out, don't hide them away. Let the world see them!" he called. She laughed off the calls for her to reveal all. She wasn't getting paid for this first photo session. She only got in front of the camera as a joke after watching her friend from the bar go topless in her own shoot, so she wasn't ready to go all the way.

Within months, Heather was in a different studio, this time in North London. She still wasn't getting paid. But she was hoping that was all about to change. The shoot was an audition for a lingerie catalog, and photographer Jeff Kaine remembers how much fun—and how desperate—the pneumatic blonde in front of his camera seemed to be. "You should hire me. I'm going to be famous one day," he remembers her calling out as she got her clothes off for the shoot. Something told him she might be right. She was still a few months short of her 19th birthday and totally inexperienced as a model. But there was certainly something special about her. "She was one of dozens of other girls, but even then she stood out," he says. "She had a sensational figure, but also a potent sexual allure." She got the lingerie job.

Other work flooded in. Heather was chosen to be one of the topless "Page Three girls" in one of Britain's million-selling

Sunday papers. She spent a year doing other swimwear work and a selection of racy lingerie shots. And then she agreed to a job that would come back to haunt her nearly two decades later. In 1988, Heather, now 20, flew to Germany to do the pictures for a 112-page "educational" magazine called *Die Freuden Der Liebe—The Joys of Love*. The magazine featured Heather and male model and aspiring actor, Peter Wilson. When they signed up, neither were entirely clear what the project would involve. Peter says his agent had told him it was for an "educational sex book." He was wary of anything that might be described as pornography because he didn't want to jeopardize his acting career. Heather, meanwhile, has never spoken publicly about the shoot. This is the inside story.

She and Peter were paid the equivalent of around $300 for the single day's work. Peter remembers Heather as a hard-working professional who was happy to do whatever the photographer wanted. The shoot itself was hardly erotic. The small studio was crowded and everyone was eager to get through the shots as quickly and efficiently as possible. "With Heather it was always: 'Next shot,' and we carried on," Peter says. When he wanted to call a halt at one point, she told him to "get with the program" and keep going because she knew they both needed the money. There was a tiny dressing room next to the studio, and the two models took refuge there between some shots. Wrapped up in dressing gowns and feeling vulnerable, they both talked about their childhoods, their lives to date and their goals. Even then Heather saw herself as "a survivor" who had to face the world on her own, says Peter. "I've had a tough life and therefore I do what I do. Don't question me," she told him when he tried to give her advice on her career. Then it was back in front of the cameras with the stockings, the whipped cream and the sex aids.

What happened at the end of the day gives another clue as to the real Heather Mills. "It was usual after a day's modeling to end with me going out with the girl, taking her for a meal, to a club and then having sex," says Peter. But while Heather had been utterly provocative in the studio, her co-star says she shut right down afterwards. Perhaps she already realized that Peter Wilson would never be any use to her. Perhaps she was just tired. But when the shoot ended, Heather went back to her hotel room alone.

The fee for the German job didn't pay many weeks' rent back in London and Heather struggled to move out of the "glamour ghetto." She had wised up to the fact that everyone had been lying when they had said that some topless pictures could open the door to a mainstream modeling career. Right from the start she had known that the photographers were spinning a line to persuade her to work for them. But she had hoped for better from her female friends in the industry. She toughened up as she faced the reality of her situation. If she was going to survive she would need to live on her wits. She would have to exploit her looks. It meant more work as a hostess, serving drinks and chatting up customers in London's sexual underworld.

Heather started off with a new job as a cocktail waitress in a Soho bar called Bananas. It was the busiest place she had worked and Heather was a hit from the first night. She had bought a tiny beige leather mini skirt to show off her long legs and a small top to showcase her breasts. She still loved dancing, so she was happy to take to the floor when she wasn't serving drinks or behind the bar. Other co-workers remember the youngster as being "bubbly" and "enthusiastic" and "great fun." She was always ready to dash out to a nearby convenience store if the bar ran dry of any drinks—and she loved the stir she made as she crossed the London streets in her skimpy nightclub clothes. At closing time she often chilled out with the club's DJ, a man called Denys, and his sister Dianna. One night, their other brother came by for a late night drink. His name was Alfie Karmal—Heather was smitten.

At first glance he was hardly an ideal date. He was some seven years older than Heather. He was in the process of getting divorced. He had two children to support and he was living in a single room even smaller than the one Heather's mother had rented when she had first moved to London. But Heather couldn't take her eyes off him. He was handsome and seemed calm, cultured and sophisticated. When he asked her out she said yes without a second thought. For the next six months, Heather and the Karmal clan all got along famously. She introduced Alfie to Fiona and to her mother, and she met Alfie's parents, his former wife and his two children. Everyone bonded. Feeling happy in her personal life made Heather feel more confident about her career. She was certain that with Alfie at her side, she could get out of the glamour world and become a proper model. For once she was right.

It was Alfie who spotted the Model of the Year competition being run by liquor firm, Cinzano. He persuaded Heather to enter and cheered as she came second in the first set of heats. A month later, she came first in the regional finals. In the final itself, she was outclassed by the other girls and was out of the running. She vowed to learn from the experience.

Meanwhile, Alfie was busy planning lots of other opportunities for his beautiful young girlfriend. He arranged for some more photo shoots and sent pictures to as many magazines and newspapers as he could find. He entered other competitions on Heather's behalf—and for a while it seemed to pay off. Heather was short-listed in one national newspaper's Dream Girl competition, found work presenting short videos for a marketing company and modeled clothes for a mail order catalog. She even got an agent.

Heather's legs were her big selling point. They seemed endless. She was still a fitness fanatic and kept herself in great shape so her calves and thighs were toned to perfection. She was never let down by a bad tan after weekly visits to the sunbed. Her legs made her a natural for swimwear jobs and for one catalog, Heather even got to travel so the pictures could be taken on a real, palm-fringed beach.

But while she doesn't like to admit it now, big money jobs were actually few and far between. And not everything she tried to do in the quiet patches between them was very successful. One day, for example, Dianna got Heather an audition for a job as a dancer on a television program called *The Hippodrome Show*. A bank of casting directors and choreographers sat in a London theater watching the candidates. Heather didn't shine. "She was trying so very hard—but it was excruciating," remembers Dianna. "She stood out like a sore thumb among all the professional dancers. We were squirming in our seats." Other rejections also hit Heather hard. The swimsuit job hadn't opened as many doors as she had hoped. So she went from casting to casting and remembers the brutality of every dismissal.

"You're too short."

"You're too busty."

"You're too old."

"You're too young."

"Your hair's not right."

"You're just not what we're looking for."

One model scout even told Heather she was too fat—and this was long before heroin chic and size zero came into vogue. When the work was hard to find, Heather admits she made extra money in dozens of different ways. She tried sales jobs, went back to the bars, even moved in with Alfie's sister to help look after her children. She and Alfie were trying to save as much money as possible so he could move out of his single room apartment and they could live together. They did so around six months after they met.

Years later, when relations between them all had soured, Dianna and Alfie both said some terrible things about Heather. In different interviews, both would claim she was always telling lies. For example, Alfie mentions a time she agreed to drive him home from a night out after he had drunk too much. She had said she had passed her test, he claims. But after they lurched their way down the street and almost drove into a brick wall,

Heather admitted she had never even had a single lesson. Meanwhile, Dianna remembers Heather telling her family about the great grades she had achieved in her high school exams. But when she asked for more detail she eventually realized that Heather hadn't taken the exams, let alone passed them with flying colors.

"I soon began to realize that Heather had difficulty with reality and telling the truth. She told me so many fibs that if she said it was raining, I would have checked," Alfie said years later. But he agrees that there was never anything malicious in Heather's exaggerations. "She desperately wanted people to like her, so she built herself up into something she thought they wanted her to be. There was always a bit of truth to her fiction." Alfie is also the first to admit that Heather's "lies" could easily be explained by her awful childhood. "Most children are told not to lie and this shapes their conscience. But if you are told it is alright when you are very young, lying becomes an automatic response," he said. He had been horrified early in their relationship when Heather had told him how often her dad had forced her to lie to the bailiffs and their landlords when she was growing up. He had laughed along with her after photoshoots when she had managed to persuade photographers and booking agents that she was several years older than her true age. He knew she did what she had to do to get by.

Dianna agreed that most of Heather's exaggerations could be explained away as bravado. They were really white lies, designed to make her seem more mature or interesting. Back in those early days of their relationship and friendship, neither Alfie nor Dianna thought that Heather was really keeping any big secrets from them. Today they know different.

Denise Hewitt was one of the many sexy young women in Heather's circle in the mid-to late 1980s. Denise, who would ultimately marry into England's hugely wealthy Berkeley Homes empire, was born in Newcastle, near where Heather spent most of her childhood. She says she felt an instant connection with

Heather—another working-class girl who traded on her looks to escape poverty, boredom and abuse. As a teenager Denise says she too was happy modeling swimwear and lingerie and doing the occasional "glamour" session for photographers. "The pay was good and there was a group of northern lasses who all got on well," she says. Heather was a favorite and she always made Denise smile. "She was a bundle of energy back then. She is such a determined girl. She was doing exactly the same as the rest of us, but she would always claim she was being paid more. She had an 'anything you can do I can do better' attitude, but it was hard to dislike her."

Denise has said how easy it was for any of the girls in the Soho set to move from topless modeling to something with a harder edge. "It was impossible to miss what was going on," she says. "Some of my friends would disappear for days on end, then come back waving wads of cash and talking about private jets and villas and yachts. They all said it wasn't a big deal." After agonizing about her own choices, Denise says she followed her friends' lead. And she refuses to be ashamed. "It wasn't that hard to make the leap. I'd had a lot of boyfriends who had treated me very badly, while all my clients were complete gentlemen."

Many of the girls in Denise's new world say that it was essential to have a mentor on hand if they were to earn the maximum amount of money for their efforts. Ros Ashley, a long-term mistress of arms dealer Adnan Khashoggi, says this was the role she performed for Heather. Ros told *News of the World* reporter Ross Hall that she knew straight away that Heather had the kind of figure that could drive men wild—and make her a lot of cash. Ros says she took her young protégé shopping in the Joseph store on ritzy Sloane Street, where she encouraged Heather to spend what seemed like a huge amount on a short, show-stopping dress. "You have to speculate to accumulate," she told the youngster. "She didn't know anyone back then and she had terrible dress sense. I felt like Henry Higgins, giving her modeling tips and telling her to find a proper agency," she added. Ros says that after introducing Heather to a wealthy Lebanese businessman at lunch one day, she lost touch with her for a while. But a few months later, Ros remembers a big party she helped set up in London's five-star Dorchester Hotel.

"It was the early Nineties and Prince Turki bin Nasser had asked me to arrange for the girls to come. On occasions like that I would invite my friends, but I would also call up the madams and get extra girls lined up." She says Heather was among the group of girls who turned up one night. Ros says she remembers another time when she claims Heather was at a lavish party at Khashoggi's extraordinarily luxurious home in Marbella, Spain. Plenty of prostitutes—known as "flower girls" by their rich Arab employers—were in the villa at the same time and the money flowed freely.

Ros admits she collected up to $6,000 in cash for every evening she helped arrange. The newest girls could get $2,000. This was only the beginning. After proving themselves at their first few parties, the girls started to collect even more. Today they speak of the jewelry, the designer clothes and the first class plane tickets. Oil money meant Middle Eastern men and their entourages had plenty of cash to throw around and plenty of empty hours to fill. Their favorite companions could be flown to any number of five-star hotels or private homes around the world. They would be chauffeured to the best boutiques for shopping sessions right out of *Pretty Woman*. Then they would return to find little boxes from Tiffany, Asprey or Van Cleef & Arpels by their bedsides.

"After your first few parties, money was thought to be too crude, so the currency became gifts. Gifts you could only risk selling years later when you had left the inner circle," says one of the party girls of the era. She confirms that the sex was supposed to be wild and enthusiastic. The girls had to make their hosts believe that they were there for the fun, not the financial rewards. They also had to follow their exotic hosts' equally exotic sense of hospitality. If this meant being shared by several men, then that was how it was. Sharing each other was also part of the deal.

Bisexual displays were encouraged—and triggered false rumors years later that Heather had a lesbian past.

Above all else the girls in the party set had one final set of rules to follow. They had to be entirely discreet and live by a code of silence about what they did, where and when. This cloak of secrecy protects many of them to this day.

For her part, Heather continues to deny playing any role in this secret world. She says the stories are "vile allegations and lies" and says that one day she will sue anyone who makes them. In her autobiography, *A Single Step* she suggests other explanations for the missing years in this part of her life. While she doesn't produce any images to back it up, she describes trips to the Caribbean to model swimwear. She mentions year-long photographic jobs in Paris where she was "the face" for an un-named makeup company's products and earned $3,000 a day. Few people are convinced and many are saddened by the smoke-screen they say Heather feels obliged to hide behind. "The tragedy is that Heather wasn't doing anything illegal and it's not as if countless other pretty girls haven't done the same since the dawn of time," says one former friend who enjoyed the high life with her in London. "She has always done what it takes to survive and she should celebrate that rather than be ashamed of it."

Others are adamant that Heather's own accounts of life back then don't add up. In 2006, the English newspaper, *The News of the World* claimed it had "sworn affidavits" from Khashoggi's private secretary Abdul Khoury. He worked for Khashoggi from 1977 until 2005. "One of my duties was to look after Mr. Khashoggi's guests, which would include looking after vice girls who were invited to see him." Abdul claims he once arranged plane tickets so Heather could fly from London to Marbella for a party. Adnan Khashoggi himself has neither confirmed nor denied exactly what went on in those heady days in the late 1980s and early 1990s. When he was interviewed on U.S. television by Daphne Barak in July 2006, his answers were far from conclusive.

"Have you ever paid for sex?" she asked.

"Let me see, if I'm under oath I will say yes. If I'm not, I will say no."

Barak made her next question more specific. She asked if he had ever paid Heather Mills to have sex with him or his guests in Marbella.

"Who cares?" he replied.

Barak asked the question again.

"Who cares?" Khashoggi repeated, before moving the conversation on.

At the time in question, Khashoggi was one of the richest men in the world and a famously big spender. Being in his company would have been an intoxicating experience for someone like Heather who had been struggling to survive all her life and had very little to lose. But would it be enough to be a play thing for a man or group of men who would always be hunting for newer, younger models? It seems Heather was well aware of the risk. She always had a plan. Ros says Heather was always more focused than the rest of their crowd. She was always looking at the bigger picture. "I remember that she always, always wanted to go to the gym," she says. "She was super-fit. We all kept ourselves in shape, but sometimes it was as though Heather was competing with the men. She was in such good health because she never did drugs and she really didn't drink. The girls would be getting a bit smashed and having a good gossip over a bottle of champagne and she'd be on the treadmill." It wasn't just Ros who was impressed by Heather's endless desire to better herself. Her efforts were to pay off very quickly indeed.

The man who made the difference was a super-rich, 47-year-old married diplomat named George Kazan. The father-of-two says that he immediately saw that Heather was "special" and says she had "both beauty and brains." He saw her as a challenge and he turned into her next Henry Higgins. "I taught her to appreciate the finer things in life. It was an amazing lifestyle for her, another world from what she was used to. But she was a quick learner," he told *Sunday Mirror* reporter Louise Hancock years later. Kazan says he rented an apartment for Heather in Paris (she told Alfie that her new home was being paid for by an unnamed cosmetics company) and that a lengthy, on-off affair began. "She did do some modeling when I knew her in Paris, but it didn't bring in the kind of money she was after," he says. "She was a minor model. She needed something else. And that something was me."

Or at least it was for a while. George says that at the start, Heather seemed happy spending her days in the gym, the hair salon and the spa. She seemed content to fill her time with a little shopping and some lunches with the other girls. But as usual, she got bored very fast. And while she wasn't entirely motivated by money, she was obsessed by status. Being a rich man's mistress was a step up the ladder from being just another "flower girl" at an exotic party. But being the other woman still meant living a life in the shadows. Heather wanted her time in the sun. She didn't like having to be in private dining rooms, kept away from prying eyes. She hated having to socialize in a group so no one would know who she was really with. As she mingled in the rich salons of Paris, she recognized the power and the influence that all the wives had, even if everyone knew that their husbands were keeping younger models elsewhere in the city. Heather wanted that power for herself. But deep down she knew she would never get it.

When it became clear that George would never get a divorce, the gloves came off. He talks of arguments, angry phone calls and Heather's threats to reveal all to his wife. But however hard she fought, Heather knew she could never win this battle. Like every other former mistress, she knew she could be cast out and made homeless overnight. So she decided to jump before she was pushed. One day she might hope to find a rich and powerful man of her own. But for now, her Parisian adventure was over. She had to leave the city fast.

Alfie took her phone call at their home outside London. It was December 1988 and Heather was in tears. She begged him to pick her up at the ferry port the following morning. She was coming home in a hurry and she needed to see him. Two days later, she asked him to marry her.

Alfie didn't say "yes" right away. He was worried that they had drifted apart during Heather's long absences. He wanted a wife who would share every aspect of his life, not one who would always be at the end of a long-distance phone line. He was also concerned about the clear discrepancies in the accounts Heather had given him about her time overseas. Had the white lies and exaggerations of old developed into something more serious? And why had the woman who had been so distant suddenly become so determined to get married? What he didn't know was that Heather's marriage proposal was a knee-jerk response to the rejection she had faced in Paris. She wanted a fresh start and some calmer times after the turbulence of the jet set. She was acting on impulse as usual. But she was convinced that settling down with Alfie was the right thing to do.

By the time Heather turned 21 in January 1989, she and Alfie had set the date for their wedding and Heather had thrown herself into the preparations. The big day was going to be May 6th. Heather and her sister had a fantastic time making arrangements for the venue, the flowers, the entertainment, the food and, of course, the dress. For a very brief period, Heather allowed herself to be truly happy. She wanted to forget the bright lights and dubious charms of her secret world in Paris, St. Tropez and beyond. But life was about to spring yet another terrible surprise.

"Are you alright? What is it?" Heather stopped dead in her tracks. Her mother had just told her she was going into hospital.

"It's nothing serious. Just a minor operation," Beatrice said lightly. She said the leg she had nearly lost all those years ago had started to cause even more problems. It had always ached and there had been regular flare-ups when the joints got inflamed. But in recent months, one of her old scars had opened up again and seemed to be badly infected. The doctors wanted to do some more corrective surgery to try and clear it all up. Heather left her mother's house feeling like a child again. Whenever she thought back to her mother's accident, she remembered all the anger and the tension of her old home. She remembered the pain of being abandoned by the woman she had loved and admired. Fortunately, when she and the rest of the family visited Beatrice in the hospital in February 1989, everything seemed to have gone well.

"I'll be home in a couple of days," Beatrice said.

But she wasn't. Heather remembers her next visit to the hospital. She remembers going to her mother's ward and finding an empty bed. Something had happened, the nurses told her. Beatrice had been taken to the intensive care ward. No one knew exactly how serious it might be. Heather, Fiona, Shane and Charles stalked the hospital corridors as they waited for news. After several hours of worry, they were told that the surgeons had found blood clots in Beatrice's heart and lungs. She needed another emergency operation to try and remove them.

When the doctors said the family could finally go in and see Beatrice, she was unconscious and breathing through a respirator. A little while later, they were called out of her room while more tests were done. Then the doctors broke the news. Beatrice had slipped into a coma. If she came round at all the likelihood was that she would be severely brain-damaged. The next few hours would be critical.

"What do we do?" Heather, Fiona and Shane had just been given the worst possible update. Their mother had been declared braindead. The doctors needed to know when they should turn off the life support machine. It was the kind of question no child should ever be asked. But before they spoke, one of the machines at the head of Beatrice's bed started bleeping a terrible warning. Then another. Heather saw her mother die in front of her eyes. She rushed forward to touch and hold her one last time in her hospital bed.

"It's so unfair, it's so unfair," she and Fiona screamed through the tears as they hugged Charles and Shane. This was the woman they had lost for so many crucial years. The woman they were only now starting to rediscover. It wasn't right that she had been taken away from them once again.

The funeral took place in Chelsea. Heather's wedding plans were on hold. The joy of her recent 21st birthday celebrations were forgotten. But amidst all the sadness of her mother's burial, she was to learn an important new lesson. The first message came from the other mourners. Heather and her family had expected a few of their mother's fellow counselors from her hospital to turn up, and possibly some of her patients. In the end nearly a hundred patients crowded into the beautiful, West London church. Many were crying. All told extraordinary stories of the love and care that Beatrice had shown them.

After the funeral, Heather spent a few days with her grandmother. They talked non-stop about Beatrice, and Heather heard for the first time about her mother's childhood, her ambitions and her early accomplishments. It seemed as if the woman Heather had only ever seen defer to unpleasant men had kept most of her talents hidden. She could have achieved so much more, Heather learned. And in her work at the hospital, she had finally started to fulfill her potential. It was clear that Beatrice had finally found her true role, caring for the sick and the dying. She had proved that it was possible to change. People had loved her. As she headed back to London from her grandmother's house, Heather stored all these facts away in her mind. She wondered if one day she too might have the courage to do something wonderful.

It isn't easy to put the final touches on a wedding when you are caught up in a fog of grief. Heather says she sleepwalked through the two months between her mother's funeral and her own big day in church. At times she had thought she should delay the service. But she knew how excited her mother had been about the wedding. She was her eldest daughter. Wherever

Beatrice was, Heather wanted to make her feel proud. The wedding took place on a sunny day in a church in Stanmore, in the northwest corner of London. Afterwards, everyone headed to a reception at the nearby Cloisters Wood Country Club. Guests remember Alfie's emotional speech when he said he was the luckiest man in the world. They remember Heather's own words and the heart-felt reference to her absent mother.

As she sat at the top table during the speeches, Heather could see an empty chair ahead of her. Charles had been in the church and had come on to the reception to toast the newlyweds. But after a few sips of champagne, she had watched him leave just before the meal. He had thought the wedding was taking place too soon after Beatrice's death. Heather would never see him again.

She and Alfie honeymooned in St. Lucia and returned to an entirely new world. Alfie's computer business was booming. He bought a four bedroom home with a swimming pool out in the fast-growing commuter town of Hoddesdon in Hertfordshire. He and Heather felt like children, rattling around such a big property and living amidst some seriously rich neighbors. Unfortunately, Heather couldn't relax amidst the country club set. She was still just 21, and she wasn't ready to settle down. She hated the idea of being a stay-at-home housewife, spending her husband's money and wasting her days at beauty salons and spas. She was desperate to retain her independence and keep her mind alive. And this meant earning money of her own.

After talking over an endless series of plans with Alfie and their friends, Heather decided to go back to modeling—but this time as an agency boss rather than a model. She figured too many of the existing agencies were run by people who didn't really understand the business. She was certain that as an ex-model herself, she could add real extra value for clients. After weeks spent chasing business on the phone and wooing models, photographers and casting directors, Heather decided she was ready to set up shop. She joined forces with a friend and set up the ExSell agency.

Heather proved to be a tough boss. She made it clear to her models that she would always go the extra mile to represent their interests. She would take all their hopes and dreams on board when she allocated jobs. But, she would expect total professionalism in return. Still fiercely anti-drugs and only a very occasional drinker, Heather said she wouldn't accept models who turned up late for bookings, let themselves get out of condition or expected to work when they were clearly tired, hung-over or stoned. "Your reputation is my reputation—and I'm not prepared to risk that," she told them.

In return, Heather managed to build up an enviable success rate. She was forensically careful in the way she selected models for each casting. Only those who clearly met the brief would be sent out—and clients appreciated it. After a few months, ExSell started to represent photographers as well as models and won some big contracts with magazines and retail stores. Heather loved the cut and thrust of the business world. She thrived in meetings and enjoyed negotiations. A trade magazine called Heather "the smartest, chicest and toughest agency manager you are likely to meet." She loved it. If a potential client turned her down, she would work every hour to change their minds. Winning business became an obsession. The more she won, the more she felt she had to prove.

As they were both working long hours, Heather and Alfie started to see less and less of each other. Her sister-in-law, Dianna, says Alfie was still "besotted" with his young wife. But would their careers take their lives in different directions?

Before they had time to answer the question, Heather realized she was pregnant. She and Alfie were ecstatic and Heather says the timing couldn't have been better. This was her cue to step away from her business and explore a very different, domestic role. She and Alfie would be the perfect parents she had never had. She decided to sell her share of the ExSell agency and prepared for a whole new adventure. But it never came. Heather's health deteriorated badly and after thinking she had miscarried, she was diagnosed as suffering a particularly complex ectopic pregnancy. "We both cried our eyes out at the hospital," Alfie remembers after they were told that their baby would never be born.

Back at home, the pair both reacted to the situation in very different ways. Alfie threw himself into his work. He had moved on from the computer world into a host of other businesses and was about to open a night club. All his attention went to that. Heather rattled around their big empty house feeling terrible about herself. She felt her body had let her down. So she wanted to change it. Less than two months after losing her baby, she booked herself into a London clinic to have a breast reduction. She went down two cup sizes to a 32C, the size she had always wanted to be. But she was still unhappy.

"I'm going back to modeling."

It was the day after the operation and Heather and Alfie were making an effort to spend time together. He took the news in silence. Heather was changing her bandages and she certainly didn't look ready to go back in front of the cameras.

"Let's just wait and see," he said, finally. Both of them knew that Heather needed a more immediate boost to take her mind off her troubles. They decided a vacation could do the trick—though they weren't planning to go away together. The following evening they remembered that Alfie's ex-wife Annie was about to take their sons skiing in Yugoslavia. Heather asked if she could join them. She and Annie had been friends from their first meeting and the boys had always liked their sporty step-mother. They said they would love to teach her to ski. On a whim, Heather also called an old friend from work, the photographer John Davis. She thought he might want to do some pictures of her in the snow to kick-start her modeling career. As usual Heather wasn't going to miss a single chance for self-promotion. John said yes. So Heather booked her flight to the Balkans. Nothing would ever be the same again.

CHAPTER FIVE
Falling in Love Again

M aybe it was the weather. Maybe it was the fresh air. Maybe it was just the fact that she was finally having a break from Britain. Whatever the reason, Heather fell head over heels in love with both skiing and Yugoslavia. The group had picked the perfect week for their trip. The sun shone every day and Heather couldn't believe the contrast between the rich blue skies and the deep, white snow. She also loved the challenge of learning a new sport from scratch. She still had stitches in her breasts and wasn't fully fit after her failed pregnancy. But she was determined to do as much as she could. Heather Mills was never going to stay on the bunny slopes for long.

The group were staying in Bled, a long-established Tyrolean-looking resort near the historic town of Ljubljana. From their hotel they could look out one way and see the Julian Alps and then the other to see the proud church standing on a picture-perfect island on the middle of Lake Bled. Heather's travels had already taken her to plenty of places. But she didn't think she had ever seen anywhere as perfect as this. The whole group also fell in love with the locals. Heather's photoshoot had certainly gotten them noticed—she was posing in swimwear in the snow. And everyone seemed to want to come up and talk to her afterwards. Every night in their hotel's bar and game room, Heather, Annie, John and the boys mingled easily with locals and vacationers alike. A getaway really did seem to be curing all of Heather's ills. She didn't want this one to end.

The day before she was due to fly home, Heather got involved in a conversation with one of the ski instructors she had seen on the slopes and in the hotel bar. His name was Milos. He was hugely proud of his country's turbulent history and had big dreams for its future. Heather was fascinated by his patriotism and his passion. She realized how attractive it was when people had a cause.

"You should see Ljubljana before you leave. It is the most beautiful city. I can take you there," he said, as they shared another drink.

"But I'm going home tomorrow."

"We can go for dinner tonight."

On a whim, Heather decided to take this man up on his offer. He seemed a genuinely nice guy and because everyone in the resort knew him, she was certain he would act like a gentleman. As it turned out, both Milos and Ljubljana lived up to all her expectations and more. The ancient city was enchanting. Milos walked Heather around the squares, along the river and across its unique set of ancient bridges. They looked up at the castle on the hill and headed into a series of tiny, smoky pubs where they slowly learned more about each other. Milos had recently split up with his girlfriend. Heather told him how unhappy and confused she was feeling at home. Heather said goodbye to Milos with a single kiss goodnight. She flew home the next morning as planned. But she had left her heart behind.

Back in Britain, she realized that Milos was never far from her thoughts. "This is ridiculous," she told herself. "I hardly know him. All we have done is spend one evening talking." But still she thought of him. She told a few close girlfriends about her feelings and they told her to grow up. "He's a ski instructor. He probably takes a different woman out to the city every week," one of them told her. "It wasn't even a proper holiday romance. You need to forget him." But she couldn't. Acting on impulse, Heather told Alfie that she was desperate to go skiing again. She booked another ten day trip to Bled, this time on her own. The moment she arrived, she called Milos—fully prepared for him to be with another woman or even to have forgotten all about her. Instead, he whooped with joy when he heard her voice and arrived at her hotel door within the hour. They were together practically 24-hours-a-day for the next ten days.

Heather says she learned everything about him in that period. She learned how kind and patient he was. She saw how deeply he thought about everything from politics to patriotism. She found out what made him laugh. He told her what had last made him cry. She met his friends and she felt entirely comfortable in his life. It didn't matter for a moment that he didn't have more than a few coins in his pocket at any one time. The battered old VW van which had taken her to Ljubljana on their first date actually broke down for good on her second visit. Milos clearly didn't have any money to fix it properly, let alone replace it. But that didn't matter to him, so it didn't matter to her. She was in love with him, she knew. After just ten days. More than this, she knew she wanted to give up everything to be with him. Her marriage, her big suburban home, her swimming pool, her modeling career. Everything could be left behind in England. Heather wanted to start all over again in Yugoslavia.

Not surprisingly, Alfie saw things differently. So did his sister, Dianna, who couldn't believe that her brother was being dumped for what she called "a penniless ski instructor." Alfie was also distraught with the speed at which Heather ended their marriage. "She just took off and left. She came back on Saturday, and by Monday morning she had gone," he remembers. "When I got home from work that night the bedroom looked as if it had been trashed. Wallpaper had been scraped off the walls by her suitcases as she dragged them down the stairs, and she had slammed the front door so hard in her haste to leave the glass panel next to it had shattered. At first I thought we had been broken into." There was more. "I later found out that she had gone straight to a car dealership and sold her £20,000 BMW convertible for £12,000 cash, and all her Cartier jewelry," says

Alfie. Over the coming months the pair started fast-track divorce proceedings and formally ended their relationship relatively painlessly. And for all his shock at the way Heather had left him, Alfie was still prepared to give her credit for their good times. He would never deny that she had a good heart.

"She is the kind of woman who can take you to the most incredible highs," he said. "She has a very tender, caring, compassionate side, which is what makes her so attractive, though she also has this other fiery, confrontational side. Part of me feels sorry for Heather. I don't hate her. All she has ever wanted is to be loved, cared for and liked," he said. Over in Yugoslavia, Heather would have been the first to agree.

By the end of March 1991, Heather had thrown herself into Yugoslavian life with enthusiasm. The ski season was coming to its close, but she rushed to complete the first stage of her training to become a ski instructor. She wanted to be able to work as soon as possible the following winter. Milos had been offered a summer job teaching tennis on an island off the coast of Croatia, so they both headed over there together. Heather earned a little bit of money teaching aerobics while she tried to work out what to do next. What she didn't know was that political storm clouds were building up back on the mainland.

The early 1990s were terrible times for Yugoslavia, a country soon to be torn apart by ethnic cleansing and war. The passionately political Milos talked endlessly about the changes and Heather was desperate to understand more about the ethnic, cultural and historical tensions in her adopted homeland. Yugoslav President Slobodan Milosevic was determined to hold his fractured country together. But the Serbs, the Croats, the Slovenians, the Bosnians and all the other factions were after independence.

"There's going to be a war," one of Heather's new friends told her. But that simply seemed improbable. Slovenia seemed to be such a relaxed and comfortable place. It was fast-becoming a top tourist destination. Fiona had just booked a flight for a visit and Heather couldn't wait to show her around. But it turned out the pessimists were right. War was just around the corner. It was on the last day of Fiona's trip that they heard a rumor that Serbian forces had invaded Slovenia. She had only just managed to get on a plane home before the airport closed after a major security alert. Heather remembers the phone call she had from her sister the next day. Fiona begged her to leave the country as fast as she could. The news reports in London were saying it was much too dangerous to stay.

But after hanging up, Heather looked at Milos and their friends in Ljubljana and knew she could only leave if they did. This felt as if it was her fight too. She vowed to stick with the others and see it through. For a couple of days, everything seemed calm. It appeared as if the previous invasion rumor had been just that. But then the tanks really did start to arrive. Ljubljana was suddenly full of makeshift barricades, the country's borders were said to be closing and everyone who could was being urged to flee. That included Heather and Milos. They packed what they could into their current car and headed for the Austrian border. Once they had crossed it, Heather put her foot down and said they should continue on to England. They could plan their next move from there.

An exhausted Heather parked the now battered and dirty Fiat outside her sister's flat in South London, and rang the bell. When Fiona saw her they both started to cry. After hugging Milos as well, Fiona left the pair alone to recover from their journey. But neither Heather nor Milos could relax. Over the next few days they bought every newspaper they could and watched every news broadcast to find out what was happening back in Yugoslavia. But the conflict seemed to be passing most people by. It was barely mentioned on television and almost completely ignored in print. Heather and Milos rang their friends in Ljubljana as often as they could, but often those on the ground were none the wiser. What Heather and Milos did know was that they weren't alone in worrying. They contacted the London office of Adria Airways, the Slovenian national carrier, to see if the airports were open and they struggled to get through. It seemed that desperate Slovenians were jamming the airline's phone lines because they couldn't think of anywhere else to go for information about the crisis. Heather decided to take action on two different fronts.

First, she thought people needed a single point of contact for information and advice. Secondly, she felt this could help get the media interested in the conflict. She and Milos set up what they called the Slovenian Crisis Centre. Whole groups of Slovenians would meet at each others' homes to try and co-ordinate a response to the crisis. Meanwhile Heather tried to persuade the media that the problems in Yugoslavia were more than just a little local difficulty.

She didn't get very far. The news editors were abrupt and unhelpful. They couldn't see a British or even an international angle to the story. And at that point Heather was too inexperienced in the ways of newspapers to find one. It was a frustrating and frightening time, she says. And it was made much worse because both she and Milos were fast running out of money. In desperation she went back to her old agency to see if they had any modeling work. The bosses spotted straight away that she had had a breast reduction. They approved. Heather was taken back on to their books and started to win a few jobs. None would exactly set the world on fire and she was hardly threatening the super-models or anyone on the cover of Vogue. But she at least had enough cash to survive. Milos wasn't so lucky. British immigration was tough on illegal workers and ski instructors were hardly required in central London. So as news reports said the focus of the Balkan war had moved towards Croatia, he decided to go back to Slovenia. Heather promised to follow as soon as she her next job was over.

For the next six months, she tried to settle in Slovenia, but rushed back to London whenever a well-paid job came up. The "glamour girls" and the "flower girls" from Heather's old set say there was plenty of lucrative work available. They say there was plenty of money to be made by pretty, determined women who were free to fly off to be with a client at a moment's notice. But wherever work took her, Heather found her mind was always on her friends in the Baltics. Ljubljana had escaped without much damage in its short brush with the Serbs. But down the coast Croatia was suffering badly. Heather remembered the idyllic month she had taught aerobics in the Croatian hotel. She had made lovely friends there. She couldn't bear to think of how much they might be hurting. As the months passed, Heather became as obsessed as Milos with the politics of the region. And back in London, she simply couldn't understand why no one else seemed to care.

She got on the phone to the papers day after day, passing on stories from her friends about hospitals being bombed, churches razed to the ground, old people and children massacred or made homeless as the Serbs marched on. But only the BBC's World Service seemed to cover the story. Increasingly angry, Heather shifted up a gear. She started lobbying politicians. She rang her own Member of Parliament and any others she could think of. She even rang Downing Street and asked to be connected to Prime Minister Margaret Thatcher. Unsurprisingly, her call wasn't put through. With so few people willing to pick up the story, Heather sometimes felt as if she was going mad. It seemed to so important to her. The line between good and evil was so clear. But no one else would see it. "Should I just give up?" she asked her sister after yet another depressing and fruitless day on the phone to the papers. Maybe it doesn't matter after all, she was thinking. Maybe if I just ignore it, like everyone else, it will go away.

"You'll never give up," was Fiona's simple response. She knew her sister too well. She knew that Heather couldn't walk on the other side of the street and ignore people's suffering. She was right. So Fiona wasn't surprised when Heather told her she was going to fly to Croatia itself to see what was really going on.

It was late summer in 1992 when Heather saw for herself the burned-out buildings and damaged roads. She was in Sisak, where her close friend Renata Matijasevic lived, and U.N. soldiers were everywhere. But if this was peace, then Heather had no wish to live through war. She and Renata headed out to the country one day to visit some other friends and saw whole groups of refugees shuffling slowly towards them. As they got closer, Heather spotted something unusual about the people. There were old people and young children but no one in between. "The men have probably been killed, the women raped," she was told later when she asked about it. Heather saw something else for the first time that afternoon. A red stick in the middle of one of the roads. "The U.N. put it there. It means there's a landmine. We'll go 'round it," Renata said as Heather held her breath in fear. It seemed incredible that a country that had seemed so relaxed and happy just a few years earlier could now have such a terrible legacy buried within its soil.

On her way back from Croatia, Heather stopped once more in Ljubljana. Milos was living there again. And they both knew their relationship was over. Could it have lasted, if they'd stayed in the same place together for more than a few months? Heather thought they could. But when war and their financial problems got in the way, they were pushed too far apart. Now it seemed too late to bridge the gap. Their love affair had died. But they would remain friends for life. As if to prove how relaxed they were in each other's company, they both volunteered to take part in a relief effort that was being organized for Croatia. A group of students and young people had set up a series of convoys to take food, clothing and medical supplies into the country. Did Heather want to join them? She said yes, without a second thought.

Getting the unmarked truck into Croatia was the team's first big challenge. The Serbian border guards wanted to go through everything in it, including what Heather and the other drivers had in their luggage. It turned out that the authorities were particularly keen to confiscate everyone's cameras. With the U.N. watching from a distance, Heather and the team were finally waved through. *Just what is it they don't want us to photograph?* she wondered. *Just how bad can it be in the country?* Over the next few days, Heather cursed that she wasn't able to take photographs. She knew her images would have been strong enough to get the story into the British newspapers at last. She saw looted graves, desecrated churches, distraught old ladies and whole groups of tearful, homeless children.

In the coming months, Heather and the team carried out several more mercy missions. The fighting seemed to be getting more brutal, she noticed. The results of it were more apparent. The roads in particular were getting more treacherous. "The mines were everywhere and every stretch of road seemed dangerous," she says. "Many were now pitted with craters where shells and landmines had gone off." What made an even greater impression on her were the human consequences of these mines. It was then, in late 1992, that she saw her first groups of amputees.

She remembers feeling sick with horror as the locals told her that the mines weren't really designed to kill. Their primary purpose was to maim. The sickness of those who designed, manufactured and planted them was impossible to comprehend. "If the mines kill someone then it's over. People grieve and then they carry on," Heather was told. "But if the mines blow off a worker's leg, or a child's arm then the misery goes on for years. Those people become a long-term burden on their families and their communities. That's what the enemy really want. They want to weaken everyone. They want to make sure that the pain never ends." As Heather gazed out from the cab of the supply truck into the broken villages on their route, she couldn't avoid the callous logic in the landmine industry. The limbless and the disabled seemed everywhere. She had absolutely no idea how their families—who had already lost everything—could possibly cope.

As if the nightmare couldn't get deeper, Heather also remembers one other horror of those journeys into Croatia. She didn't just see the people who had survived the landmine explosions. She saw the limbs that they had left behind. The team had stopped once for a break before navigating a stretch of road that was known to be particularly dangerous. Red sticks were planted at regular intervals along the route ahead. It would take skill, courage and luck to make it to their destination. Heather stood by the van to try and calm her nerves before they set off. Then she saw them. Severed hands and arms, lying beside the road. It was the most chilling and horrific thing she had ever seen. She was 25 years old and she was overcome with anger. She vowed that when she got back to London she would do everything in her power to wipe the horror of landmines off the face of the earth.

By the spring of 1993, Heather felt as if she was living two completely different lives. There was the utterly serious Heather who rolled up her sleeves, got on the phone to newspaper columnists, politicians, commentators and charity workers to try and raise awareness of the on-going crisis in the Balkans. This Heather had become a voracious reader about other war-torn areas around the world. She focused on all the places that landmines were laid. She cried as she read of all the victims they had claimed.

The other Heather was the one who polished herself up and threw herself back into the modeling industry and the glamour world. She focused on what she ate, what she wore and how she looked. And she enjoyed it. Heather's fiercely professional attitude made her particularly employable. She was still sticking to her no-drugs, no-alcohol rules and was obsessive about arriving early and well-prepared for all her castings. It got her noticed and won her work. "She was doing really well. People knew she was hard-working and dedicated. She was a real professional and a lovely person," says photographer and old friend, John Davis. He was working with her one day in early

1993 when she found out she had won a new contract with the Gabicci fashion house. But Heather hadn't entirely shaken off her past. She talks of a well-paid swimwear job she won that spring, describing ten days spent on a luxury yacht in the Caribbean. Others talk of a similar yacht owned by a Middle Eastern Prince and populated by a group of young and beautiful women from Heather's Soho set.

Whichever yacht Heather was on, she was certainly earning more than ever before. She bought an apartment in London's young and funky West Hampstead. She bought a new car and she tried to relax. But she struggled. Sometimes all the baggage from her childhood and the memories of the Balkans could drag her down. She needed to be persuaded that having a good time in London didn't mean she was betraying her friends in Croatia. She knew she had to learn to live in the moment. The best therapy Heather has ever had was to dance. So whenever she felt depressed, she hit London's clubs with her girlfriends. She hadn't dated anyone since parting from Milos and certainly wasn't planning to settle down any time soon. That was when she met a man called Raffaele Mincione. He was going to change her life.

The pair got to talking in a big West End nightclub called Stringfellows. Heather was there with her old friend Ruth and she remembers trying to brush off all his initial approaches. She also remembers how handsome he was. Raffaele was a 28-year-old Italian who worked in an investment bank in London's financial hub—an area known as "the City." He was a bond dealer—a perfect catch for most young women. He was intrigued by Heather's indifference. She didn't want to dance with him because she said she was happy dancing with Ruth. She didn't want a drink—she said they had just bought their own. She didn't want to go on to another club after hours—they had plans of their own.

In desperation Raffaele finally asked if he could take Heather out the following night. But once more she stopped him in his tracks. She already had plans for tomorrow, she said. So she carried on dancing on her own. Raffaele's final gambit was the one that won the day. He gave Heather his number and said that if her plans fell through she should call him. He would love to take her out to dinner. As she and Ruth headed back to their apartment in West Hampstead in the early hours of the morning they couldn't stop talking about him. Ruth said she would be crazy not to at least see him again. "He's tall, he's handsome, he's Italian," she joked. "What more can a girl ask for?" So Heather gave him a call. They met for a drink, moved on to dinner and ended up in bed.

The next day, Heather couldn't believe how much she liked this intriguing new man. They had talked for hours about their childhoods and their new lives in London. Heather felt they were very different—for a start he seemed a lot more conservative than her—but they still seemed to have an instant connection. There were no silences when they were together. They sparked off each other and within days it felt as if they had known each other for years. Raffaele's next big test was to impress Fiona. He passed it with flying colors. Fiona had a new boyfriend herself and was living and working with him in Athens, Greece. Heather and Raffaele had a wonderful weekend mini-break. Relationship experts say the first time couples go away together can be make or break occasions. It is only when you are together 24-hours-a-day that you see if you are truly compatible. Heather and Raffaele didn't have a moment's problem. They remember the whole weekend passed in a blur of laughs, long conversations and great sex.

So what went wrong? Back in London, Heather suddenly went from feeling loved to feeling trapped. Looking back, she says she and Raffaele probably got too deep, too fast. His traditional Italian ways seemed restricting and Heather had never liked being told what to do. She had been enjoying her freedom in London. She didn't ever want to answer to someone.

In a total about-turn, Heather decided she wanted to see less of him, not more. Then, after a trivial argument that no one really remembers, she decided she didn't want to see him at all.

Raffaele lived in a typical City-boy's apartment near Cheyne Walk in Chelsea. On Sunday, August 8, 1993, Heather drove over there to tell him what she felt. After a brief chat in his doorway, they decided to go for a walk to clear the air. Just as she had done with Milos, Heather was determined to part amicably. She wanted to keep Raffaele as a friend. When they left the apartment, Heather and Raffaele decided to head over to the beautiful Cheyne Walk and stroll along the River Thames. But then they changed their minds. They decided instead to head north towards Princess Diana's home in Kensington Gardens. They wanted to look for the famous bronze statue of Peter Pan while they talked. With that tiny decision, Heather's fate was sealed.

CHAPTER SIX
The Accident

The emergency call came through to the West London police station moments before Heather and Raffaele reached the park. It was from one of the wealthy estates on Kensington Palace Gardens, a private road that ran alongside the royal park and housed scores of embassies and diplomatic buildings. The Diplomatic Protection Squad was committed to answering calls from embassies within two minutes. Because this call had come through from a neighboring house, the same urgency applied. Three police motorcyclists were dispatched to the scene. With sirens blaring, they headed up Kensington High Street at top speed.

Heather and Raffaele both heard the sirens as they approached Kensington Gardens. Traffic was pulling over to let the police through and their fellow pedestrians stood waiting for the all clear before crossing the road. They waited alongside them and 25-year-old Heather marvelled at how fast the two police bikes shot by. A couple of seconds later, Heather stepped forward. She didn't know a third bike was still racing towards her.

The 760cc BMW motorcycle ploughed directly into her. It was driven by 29-year-old Police Constable Simon Osborne, an experienced and well-respected member of his elite protection squad.

Onlookers say Heather, Osborne and the bike all flew into the air. Heather was pushed, then dragged nearly twenty yards down the road. Osborne and his bike hit the ground just a little bit further past them. For a split second Raffaele froze, just like all the other pedestrians beside him. Then, as everyone rushed towards the two bodies, Raffaele stopped in his tracks. There was something on the road in front of him. It was Heather's foot. In denial, he ignored it. His first priority was to check to see if Heather was alive and help her. He pushed through the crowds and crouched down at her side.

"You're going to be OK. Everything is going to be OK," he told her. But she could see the fear in his eyes. It was then that he, and the crowd, noticed the blood. Heather was bleeding almost uncontrollably. Blinking back tears, Raffaele realized the foot he had just stepped over hadn't been some awful trick of his imagination. His girlfriend had lost her leg. He knew instinctively that if they couldn't stop the bleeding, she would lose her life.

"Has anyone called an ambulance?" he shouted. As a woman in the crowd said one was on the way, he and Heather both remember hearing the most welcome voice of all.

"I'm a doctor. Let me through," a man was shouting.

The doctor had grabbed a first-aid kit from his car and he began barking orders to Heather, Raffaele and the crowd. He saved her life. It was probably the relief of knowing that help had arrived that allowed Heather to relax. She drifted in and out of consciousness several times over the next fifteen minutes on that hard roadside. At one point, when she came to and started focusing on the things around her, she saw the crowd part as Raffaele followed the doctor's instructions to collect her foot. It somehow didn't seem strange that it should be on one side of the road while she was on the other. She even felt a shadow of a smile cross her lips as a motorist drove towards her foot, threw on the brakes at the last moment, took a close look at it and decided that instead of helping he would simply reverse and drive around it. "I will never be someone like that," Heather said to herself as she closed her eyes again.

When she came around again, she watched as a new group of police officers and an ambulance crew started attending to the motorcycle rider. He was ultimately taken to the hospital and treated for bad bruising, cuts, a sprained wrist and a twisted ankle. He was able to be discharged the next day. In the back of her mind, Heather couldn't quite work out why no one except her guardian angel of a doctor was treating her. Then she closed her eyes and drifted away again. This time it would be nearly three days before she woke up.

The London Ambulance Service later explained why Heather had endured such a long wait on the roadside. The staff had seen that she was too badly injured to be taken to an ordinary emergency ward by road. She needed specialized care, so an air ambulance was scrambled to transfer her to the Mount Vernon Hospital in Northwood, Northwest London. The foot that a horrified Raffaele had picked up and carried back to her was packed in ice and transported with her. On the short flight, the crew said they thought Heather had been lost on four separate occasions. She was unconscious, desperately short of blood and had suffered major internal injuries, as well as losing her lower leg. No one could identify the life force that carried her through until she got to the safety of the trauma unit.

The surgeons at Mount Vernon are world leaders in re-attaching severed limbs. By the time Heather arrived they were ready to carry out another complex reconstruction effort. But it was immediately clear that her injuries had been too bad. Too much of the flesh had been torn away and damaged. Unlike her mother, Heather's leg could not be saved. Worse still they couldn't simply clean up her wound, stitch it and allow it to heal. Again, the trauma had been too great. They needed to cut off even more of her leg to produce a cleaner break. The operation would take nearly five hours. They warned Raffaele that his girlfriend might not survive.

Fiona was sitting at her sister's bedside when Heather regained consciousness some 36 hours later. In the previous days, she had heard the full list of her sister's injuries. Heather had a punctured lung, which was filling with a dangerous level of fluid. Her pelvis was crushed, her hip was fractured and she had broken several ribs. Much of her upper body, head and face was cut and bruised and there had been early fears that she might be badly concussed. Fiona was told that when Heather did come round she was likely to be in shock. She wouldn't know where she was and she might not even know *who* she was.

As it turned out, Fiona says Heather was completely calm when she finally opened her eyes and started talking. She could remember that there had been an accident, though the details were sketchy. She could certainly tell that she was badly ill, not least because of the pain she was in. The doctors said she wouldn't be able to take painkillers until her lung had drained. What she didn't know, of course, was that she had lost her leg. She didn't know that she was an amputee.

"How will we tell her?" Fiona and Raffaele had asked each other the question a thousand times since the accident. They hadn't found an easy answer. Doctors say that when most amputees come around after their operations, they don't feel any different. Often they only realize they have lost a limb when they are told or when they look. That was how it was with Heather. Fiona remembers how calm her sister was after the news was broken. She was in total denial. She would remain that way through two more weeks and several more operations. Fiona also remembers that in those first awful days, the only thing Heather talked about was work. She had only the sketchiest idea of how many days she had been unconscious or of how many jobs she might have missed. She begged Fiona to ring as many clients, photographers and casting agents as possible to make her apologies. She said Fiona should tell them that she would be back to work just as soon as possible.

"Heather, we need to take things slowly. We need to focus on getting you well again," the doctors told her when they overheard her discussing jobs with her sister. But Heather wouldn't listen.

As it turned out, very few of her clients needed to be told about the accident. Her story had made it on to the local television news and into most national newspapers. It was simple stuff: "Model loses leg in police chase" was a typical headline. Some of the first stories were so brief that Heather wasn't even named. But then the story grew. Well-wishers sent flowers, cards and gifts. And Heather became increasingly exasperated. She refused to accept that she needed good wishes, let alone sympathy.

She still had work on her mind, even when she was transferred to another specialist hospital and prepared for more surgery. The doctors needed to start the complex procedure of pinning a metal plate to her damaged pelvis and trying to clear up some of her other broken and crushed bones. Heather and Fiona remember how adamant she was about where the incisions would be made. She wanted the scars to be hidden so she could carry on modeling as soon as possible. She thought of all the swimwear jobs she had done in the past. Yes, she won most of them because she had such long, perfect legs. But when the shots were actually published they were often cropped at the knee. Heather was convinced she would still get work now that this was a necessity.

Heather's latest operations had taken place at an acute care center called Bishopswood in the grounds of the main Mount Vernon hospital. The nurses there were proud of how strong their new patient seemed to be. But they warned Fiona that her sister would still need plenty of support. Every patient who loses a limb breaks down or falls apart at some point, they said. Heather's moment could come at any time.

For two more weeks, Heather remained totally bedridden. She needed to use a bed pan and be washed and changed by the nurses and by her sister. Two days after her latest operation, she asked if she could finally try to walk. With help from the hospital's physiotherapists and occupational therapy teams, she was given the chance. She needed a special frame for support and it took some time for her body to regain even a little of its old flexibility. But one afternoon, less than three weeks after the accident, Heather managed to move around her room unaided. She even made it to the bathroom on her own.

It should have been her happiest moment. The nurses and doctors had applauded when they watched her get out of bed. But alone in the bathroom everything went wrong. Heather's injury was no longer something she could ignore. Her lost limb was no longer something that could be covered up by blankets. It was real. She had lost her leg. Breathing heavily, Heather washed herself in silence. She used the toilet. She pulled herself up in front of the mirror. Then she fell over.

The tiles of the bathroom floor were cold and hard. There, crumpled and in pain, the crying began. Heather curled up into a ball, sobbing and almost screaming as she finally acknowledged what had happened to her. She thought of the girl who loved to dance, to play tennis, to ski and to swim. She thought of the races she had won as a girl at school. Of all the times she had coped with life's disappointments by throwing herself into an exhausting work-out at her gym. She thought of all the places she had seen, all the experiences she had thought were still ahead of her. And she looked at the bandaged and bleeding stump at the end of her leg. Hardly able to see though her tears, Heather dragged herself out of the hospital bathroom and back towards her bed. But her nightmare continued. She realized she couldn't climb into the bed on her own. She needed help from the nurses even to do this. Heather carried on crying for the rest of that awful day. She was still in tears when darkness fell. She knew, finally, that her life had changed. She had crossed Balkan minefields without a scratch, but she had been mutilated and disabled on a sunny afternoon in Central London. She didn't think she could recover.

Fiona hadn't been Heather's only visitor over the past three weeks. Raffaele had come to the hospital almost every day as well. The pair had been wary of each other. Fiona couldn't help herself from blaming him for the accident—he couldn't help noticing. Unable to cope with the tension that developed when they were both together, Heather had told Raffaele to stay away. But after a week she relented. He cheered her up. She wanted him around.

The nurses, who had listened to Heather's heart-wrenching tears after her accident in the bathroom, were eager to encourage as many visitors as possible. However hard it sounded, they knew how important it had been for Heather to hit rock bottom. They were thrilled she was now picking herself back up off the floor. The physiotherapists issued Heather a wheelchair, and she says being in the fresh air and sunshine were an intensively important part of her recovery. That was something she would remember in the years ahead when she visited other amputees or accident victims in hospitals around the world. If no one else would help she would literally carry people out of their beds to prove that the world was still turning outside.

Back in her room, Heather sat with a pen and pad making notes about all the things she would do when she was finally discharged. The surgeons who had worked on her pelvis had been true to their words and hadn't made the scars too visible. But Heather knew that her dreams of modeling swimwear again wouldn't come true any time soon. Apart from everything else, her leg was still badly infected and the wounds were refusing to heal. So how else could she earn money? As the days passed, this was the question she kept going back to. She was on her own. She had no rich parents to bail her out, no generous employer to pay her wages while she recovered. Meanwhile, she had a mortgage to pay and a car loan to clear.

"What are these?"

"They're the forms you need for unemployment money and disability benefits."

Heather looked across the bed at the patient liaison officer who had come by to see her. She felt a strange chill as she looked at the leaflets. She didn't see herself as unemployed or disabled. It seemed so brutal that this stranger was giving her such an awful label. *You don't even know me*, she thought, angrily. *How dare you think I need your help!* Apart from the false labels, claiming money from the state went against everything Heather had ever believed in. If nothing else, her childhood had taught her self-reliance.

"I can't claim those things," she said sharply.

"But you're entitled. Everyone signs them."

"Not me."

"It's worth a lot of money."

"I don't care. I'll earn money. I don't need help from anyone."

"Well do you want me to leave the forms just in case?"

"No. I'm not changing my mind." That was it. The liaison officer left and Heather picked up her notepad again. There must be another way out of her impending financial crisis. By the end of the day, she had spotted it. The answer to all her problems was sitting in the hospital's visitors area. The newspapers hadn't let go of her story. The editors knew readers lapped up the idea of the stunning swimwear model that had been left broken in her hospital bed. So they sent reporters to Bishopswood almost every day to try and get updates from Fiona, Raffaele and the staff. But what they really wanted was an interview—and photographs—of Heather herself.

The next morning, Heather decided to grant their wishes. But on her terms. She told Fiona to put the word out that she was finally ready to talk. When every major paper sent a reporter, she called them all into her room and sprang her surprises.

The first was how she looked. The reporters say they had expected to find a pale, broken woman lying back in her hospital bed. Instead, they remember finding Heather sitting confidently in a chair, her hair glossy and styled, her makeup perfect. Their next surprise was her attitude.

Heather was playing hard-ball. She told them that she would give an exclusive, explosive interview to just one of them—with as many photographs as they wanted. The highest bidder would win the story. They had a day to come up with their best offers. As they rushed off to call their editors, Heather laughed at her own audacity.

"The press didn't expect that side of me," she remembers. "They, just knew the basic: 'dumb-model-in-hospital-loses-leg' cliché. I wanted to show I could play them at their own game." She was right. The newspaper bids were high and gave Heather enough money to last easily into the New Year. That was what she had long-since learned about money. It didn't just buy you freedom. It bought you time.

For her part, she certainly gave the paper its money's worth. She had learned a huge amount trying to get reporters interested in the Balkans crisis. She knew how important the right pictures would be. She knew that a good story needed an edge. Most important of all, she knew that sex sells.

"You do realize that no man is going to ever look at you in that way again." That's what one of the physiotherapists had told Heather two weeks earlier, after what was supposed to have been a confidence-raising visit.

"In what way, exactly?" Heather had asked her.

Embarrassed, the visitor had tried to change the subject. But when pressed, she had said that Heather's weak pelvis meant sex would be out of the question for many months. Heather had laughed. "I pity you if you only know one position," she replied. To prove it, Raffaele had started to break hospital rules by spending the night in Heather's bed. Sex hadn't been out of the question after all. And in her newspaper interview, Heather made this clear. She was desperate to show that she was still a woman. That she was still desirable.

The journalist loved it. Her exact words were re-written and exaggerated, just as she had expected. "I lost a leg but sex is as incredible as ever" ran one of her first headlines. "By the time he left, Raffaele looked in need of crutches himself," she was quoted as saying in the underlying article. It was embarrassing—especially for Raffaele—but it did the trick. Ultimately, Heather felt her self-esteem got a bigger boost than her bank balance. It would take years before she realized just what kind of Faustian pact she had made with the papers that day. She didn't realize that having invited them into her life she would now never be free of them. Nor did she know just how quickly the British press can turn upon its own.

CHAPTER SEVEN
First Steps

Putting on a brave face for journalists was one thing. Enduring the searing pain and shock of amputation was quite another. Alone in her hospital bed, Heather had the worst dreams of her life. She woke most mornings in a cold sweat, her mind racing, her future bleak. *I am a one-legged freak. What man is ever going to want me now? And when is this pain going to end?* Heather was a woman on the edge—on the edge of giving in to depression, hopelessness and despair. But in the last moments before surrendering to her fears, she always pulled herself back from the brink. *I've survived too much in my life to give in now*, she vowed. *I didn't let everything else beat me. I'll find a way through this as well.*

Fighting to survive, Heather tried to visualize a better future. She tried to picture herself somehow walking down High Street Kensington again. This time she would have an artificial leg, she knew but she was damned if it would stop men from checking out her figure. *I'll go to Harrods with my girlfriends. I'll flirt with anyone I choose. I'll learn to dance again and I will stop this pain.*

Deep in her heart Heather heard another voice. One that told her she could make something good out these bleakest of moments. *Not everyone's got your strength, Heather. Not everyone can get over things like you can. You need to show everyone that life can go on after an accident. You're the only one—the only one— who's got the power to get that message across. That's your mission. That's what you have to do.*

So she did her hair, put on full makeup and vowed to look her best the day she left Bishopswood hospital. She was unsteady on her crutches and in permanent pain. But no one would have known it to look at her. She was hiding what she felt, just as she always had. She was putting on the very best show. Proving that she could be a winner. And she had one more surprise to spring as she said goodbye to her doctors and nurses. She told them what she was doing next. She was going skiing.

A man named Mike Hammond had written to Heather while she was in the hospital. He was a fellow amputee who now ran an artificial ski slope just east of London. He wanted to reassure Heather that with the right support and the right attitude, she could carry on with all her dreams. She had called him and his encouragement had moved her to tears. That wasn't all.

A television company wanted to make a program about Heather's recovery. They wanted some dramatic footage to prove that losing a leg wasn't the end of the world. Heather knew just what to do to provide it. *I'm bloody well going to take the cameras to the ski slope,* she told herself. *The world can say what it wants about me, but it can't ever call me a victim or a coward.*

But was she a fool? Mike was particularly concerned, not least because Heather had only been walking for a matter of weeks. He was worried that she was trying too much too soon. But Heather couldn't be stopped. She gave it everything she had when the cameras came to the artificial slope. She smiled and laughed throughout the shoot. No one watching could know how much pain she was in. No one but Heather knew how raw her hips and her pelvis felt after this extraordinary display of bravery. And it would be Heather alone who would have to pick up the pieces when she found out that she had, indeed, been pushing her body too far, too fast.

This realization took several weeks to arrive. In the meantime, Heather allowed herself to believe that her nightmare was over. Years later she asked herself how she could ever have been so naïve.

Straight off the ski slope she modeled some clothes for the television program, secretly hoping that all of her old casting agents might be watching and see she was as professional and employable as before. She gave a series of interviews to talk show hosts and allowed herself to dream that she could one day carve out a career in front of the cameras. She made all the front pages after a typically ebullient Richard Branson picked her up and carried her down a flight of stairs when she had been invited to help judge the Miss U.K. contest alongside him. It was all fun and frivolous stuff.

But then it all went wrong.

Amidst all this glamour and excitement, the serious business of dealing with her injuries had continued. For a month after leaving the hospital, Heather had been going to outpatient appointments every day. In the sixth week of her supposed recovery, her doctors dropped the bombshell: her body wasn't responding to treatment. Her pains were going to get much, much worse. The nightmare was about to begin all over again.

She sat pale and silent in the doctor's office as he told her the worst. The wounds just below her knee were festering—just as her mother's had done all those years ago. Heather's leg had also developed a dangerous abscess which triggered a new series of infections. Apart from damaging her skin, the doctor said the pathogens were threatening her bones. Just as she thought she was on the road to a full recovery, the doctor broke the bad news. He wanted Heather to go back to hospital for another major operation. He needed to amputate even more of her leg.

Heather stared at the ceiling as she was prepared for surgery. There were too many tears in her eyes for her to see clearly. Too much anger in her soul for her to focus. *Why me?* she asked. *Why am I being punished? Haven't I suffered enough?* She thought back to all the bridges she had already crossed. Being beaten by her father, abandoned by her mother, exploited by what felt like every photographer and bar owner in London. *Isn't losing a leg enough, if I've committed some kind of crime? Do I need to be butchered again?*

The nurses were kind as they fussed around their patient. The operation was about to begin. And Heather was blaming herself for everything. Had she been too arrogant, thinking she was strong enough to ski so soon after the accident? Should she have listened to all those people telling her to slow down? Should she have given up and locked herself away from the world for the rest of her life?

As her trolley was wheeled into the operating theater she had never felt so weak. Or so frightened. She simply couldn't believe her life had come to this.

When she came 'round from the anaesthetic, Heather lay motionless, staring at the ceiling through cold, dry eyes. The surgeons came in and said the operation had gone well. They had cut out the infected bone, removed inches of dead skin and sealed the new wound. They said that in a few weeks she should finally be strong enough to have a proper prosthetic leg fitted. But alone in her room Heather didn't believe them. *It's just another set of lies. How many more operations am I going to have to endure?*

To make matters worse, Fiona was no longer there to lift Heather's mood. Her bosses over in Athens had been wonderful, giving her plenty of time off and saying her job would be kept open for as long as she needed. But when Heather was discharged from Bishopswood, Fiona had flown back to Greece. It was down to Raffaele, Heather's other friends, and the hospital staff to try and cheer her up. They did it by focusing relentlessly on the positives. That's what Heather would do herself for the rest of her life.

So after her first few lonely hours, she sought out stories of teenage motorcyclists who had lost legs but been back on their bikes within a year. She found out about older amputees who had been back on the golf course within months of their release from hospital. She got inspired by other people. And she realized that she had a responsibility to inspire others as well. This would indeed be her new mission in life.

Until now, Heather had been getting around using a walker, crutches or a wheelchair. Because her wounds hadn't heeled, the doctors hadn't been able to fit her with an artificial limb so she could learn to walk naturally again. Two weeks after her second operation she was told that it hadn't done the trick either. Her leg—which she decided to bluntly call her "stump"—was still red and raw. The doctors said that she had caught yet another serious infection. They said she might now need a third amputation. She would lose even more of her leg.

Her tears fell in private as she digested the news. But as she dried them she made a decision. She would not give in. She would not allow others to dictate how her future would play out. She believed in her doctors. But she wanted to take matters into her own hands.

At home with Raffaele, she began researching everything from homeopathy to acupuncture. If conventional medicine couldn't help her then she was prepared to try just about anything else. *I will walk again. I will find a way,* she told herself. *Someone, somewhere, can help me.* And after less than a week of searching, she found the answer.

The private clinic in America stood out from all the others. It was the Hippocrates Institute in West Palm Beach, Florida, and its holistic programs seemed tailor-made for Heather's situation. She booked a flight for the following week—mid-November 1992. "I have nothing to lose," she told Raffaele. *And I'm damn sure I'll make it work,* she told herself as she flew out on her own.

Wheatgrass was a central part of the clinic's dietary regimes. At first, Heather hated the taste and was skeptical about its benefits. But when you fly half way around the world in search of help, you don't let anything stand in your way. So she ate and drank everything she was told. She devoured all the information that was on offer as well. The Institute held seminars, lectures and meetings about positive thinking and healthy living. Heather took part in group therapy sessions and banished some of the demons from her troubled childhood.

She loved the "can do" attitude of America and felt invigorated under the bright Florida sun. Best of all, the infections in her leg finally started to heal. As the days passed, the puss and the weeping dried up and faded away. The scabs took hold and when they fell off, there was healthy new skin underneath them. Even the aches and pains started to fade away. Heather was able to bathe properly and swim for the first time since her accident.   After speaking to her advisors in Florida, Heather also knew she was ready for a prosthetic limb. She could finally move on.

Back in Britain in early 1994, Heather met a man who would become a friend for life. Bob Watts was the first prosthetics expert she saw after returning from Florida. Over there, she had tried out a few artificial limbs just to see how they felt. Now, she was going to learn even more about them. Bob began by fitting Heather with the kind of limb that is available for free on Britain's National Health Service. Under jeans or trousers, and with a shoe on the end, its appearance didn't matter. That was just as well. There was no hiding the fact that this most basic of limbs was false. When she wore a skirt, Heather felt it screamed "disabled" and would ultimately sap all her hard-fought confidence.

"Look, in Madame Tussauds they make wax models look lifelike. Why can't I have a limb that looks like that?" she asked Bob.

He said that she could—though it would cost a lot of money. The top of the range limbs didn't just look better, they performed better as well. Bob could fit special prosthetics that would help sports players and even swimmers. Heather decided to blow her budget on a limb that would make her mentally as well as physically comfortable.

She asked Bob to design the most lifelike model he could for her. She was amazed at the result. When she put a bandage over the joint, it was almost impossible to tell that her leg was false. She thought she simply looked like someone who had played too much tennis and was suffering a sprain. It took a bit of practice. But after a few weeks, Heather could walk without even a shadow of a limp. As she walked into a restaurant for a celebratory dinner with friends, she felt she had finally regained her poise, both literally and figuratively. She loved it.

The flexibility in her top-of-the-range leg meant there seemed to be nothing Heather couldn't do when she wore it. She tried roller blading and even booked a proper ski holiday in the snow. She fell over plenty of times on both occasions. Today, she tells wonderful stories about the time her ski, with her leg attached, fell off half way up a chair lift. The stranger who had been sitting next to her nearly passed out in shock. In London's Hyde Park, she created a similar stir when her leg twisted off while she was rollerblading. But as a crowd gathered—some to help, some to laugh—Heather simply clicked the limb back in place and carried on. She refused to give anyone the satisfaction of seeing her cry.

Heather's fitness campaign didn't end on the slopes or in the park. She was so eager to start swimming again that she agreed to be a figurehead in Britain's biggest charity Swimathon. The Olympic gold medalist Duncan Goodhew was organizing the event, and he helped Heather modify her old strokes to cope with her new body shape.

"It's just remarkable she wants to do this," he told friends, especially amazed because, while her leg was in good shape, she was still going back to the hospital for regular check-ups on her hips and pelvis.

"I've not changed. I am just someone who's had an accident and lost a leg," Heather told the press in March 1994 when she stood before them to promote the Swimathon. Then she dove into the pool and began her swim.

She continued to meet with Bob Watts to modify the fittings on her artificial limb, and he too was amazed by her. "The majority of people who have lost limbs get a lot of support from friends and family when it first happens, but, six to nine months on, depression hits. That never happened to Heather. I kept waiting for it to happen, but it never did," he says.

"This is the deal I have been given in life and I have just got to get on with it," he remembers Heather saying when he congratulated her on her progress. What he didn't know was that Heather had a secret reason for pushing herself so hard. Whenever she felt low, she remembered the amputees she had seen by the roadsides in Croatia. She didn't think for one moment that they would be getting a fraction of her opportunities. In fact, the more she thought about it, the more she wondered if Croatian hospitals fitted false limbs at all.

What's happened to all those maimed men, women and children I saw on the aid convoys? Heather knew she had to find out. She knew she had to help.

CHAPTER EIGHT

Reaching Out

Nothing had prepared Heather for the scale of the tragedy unfolding in Croatia. It was late one night in May 1994 that she rang Renata for inside information. Then she did some research of her own in London. It left her numb with shock. The UN said that up to 300,000 people in the Balkans had lost limbs because of land mines or mortars in the past few years alone.

"That's ten, a hundred times more than I'd thought," she told her friend. "Can even a fraction of them be getting the care they need?"

Renata had to say no. Croatian hospitals were overwhelmed. The few prosthetics staff they had worked flat out to fit whatever limbs they could find. But the supply was desperately limited. The work they did was a drop in the ocean.

"Renata, I'm going to come out and see things for myself. Can you join me in Zagreb?" Heather flew out of England determined to find a solution to the problem. Having faced her own mortality, she was suddenly fearless in the face of this new challenge. In Zagreb, she and Renata toured the main hospitals and spoke to their hard-pressed doctors and nurses. When they said there was nothing they could do without more government funding, Heather called upon the government. She demanded an audience with the country's Health Minister. Amazingly enough, she got one.

The minister, Dr. Vladimir Tonkovic, seemed ready to take any help Heather could offer. He admitted the country was ridiculously short of prosthetic limbs. Any extra prosthetics that Heather could ship over would be gratefully accepted, he said. But where would she get them from? Heather knew her own savings, or any money she raised doing more charity swims or walks, would hardly dent the problem. Could she organize something on the scale of Live Aid, the huge fund-raising concert that had helped alleviate African poverty back in 1985? As she flew back to London, she vowed that if that was what it took, then that was what she would do.

Heather talked the problem through with Bob when she went for her next fitting. Her leg had started to come loose and he was making her a new limb, which he promised would be tighter. The new limb would take up a large slice of her savings. But at least she knew she could donate the old one to the Zagreb hospital when she was finished with it. That was when the idea hit her.

If she was casting off an old limb that no longer fit, then how many other people across the country might be doing the same? She asked Bob. "Thousands of people. Tens of thousands. Maybe more," he told her. Apparently, everyone who had an artificial limb fitted immediately after losing a leg would see their residual limb shrink within a year. So they would all need new versions.

"What happens to the old legs?" Heather asked. Bob shrugged. He could only guess that they got put in storage or even thrown away.

"Aren't they used again by someone else?" said Heather. Bob shook his head. Limbs had to be made to measure. If anyone could be bothered, the moving parts of the old legs could be re-used. But Bob wasn't aware that this was ever done. It seemed as if the old legs simply gathered dust or got thrown away.

"Can I use your phone?" As soon as her fitting was complete, Heather wanted to find out more. Could there really be tens of thousands of unwanted limbs in the United Kingdom? It seemed ridiculous. But it turned out to be true.

Heather was told that a quirk in the way the health system was funded meant hospitals had no incentive to recycle old limbs. "If a clinic re-uses them, it loses money from next year's budget through being prudent," she was told.

"That's a crazy system. But it could help me," she said, almost to herself.

Then, she got to work. It was late June and she called everyone she knew for advice and information. She started calling the country's main hospitals. Jotting the figures down on her note pad almost made her cry. In her first afternoon's work, she had tracked down nearly a thousand spare limbs. By the end of the week, she had found five times as many. She had also managed to persuade some local charities and a few national brands to help transport them down to Bob's offices in Bournemouth. This could be turning into something really big.

But Heather hit a serious problem the moment she allowed herself to relax. The experts told her there was no point in taking 5,000 old artificial legs to Croatia. The country only really needed the key parts within them. The limbs had to be broken down and sorted before they were sent. And that was going to be a mammoth task. Heather's first idea was to call for volunteers. She was sure that plenty of people would want to help when she explained how important the job was. But how could she train them and where could they work? Bob's offices at the Dorset Orthopaedic Clinic weren't big enough. And she was in such a hurry to arrange the convoy that she wanted full-time workers rather than hard-pressed volunteers. Her old networking skills made the difference again as she got back on the phone to try and find a solution. One of the men who had worked with her on the Swimathon fundraiser seemed to have an idea. He said the voluntary work programs in jails were always looking for new charitable projects.

On a hot July day less than a week later, Heather took a deep breath and walked nervously into the high security Brixton Prison in south London. She sat with the warden and explained what she was hoping his inmates could do for her. He had reservations about the most dangerous convicts being given access to tools and blades. But he was carried away by Heather's enthusiasm. He agreed that the job could be done. He and a colleague in another prison in the Midlands signed up to the plan. Things were moving very fast.

Heather knew how important it would be to send the convoy to Croatia before winter fell. In the middle of the British summer, she gave everyone a deadline of October 30, 1994 to strive for. It was a tight schedule, but Heather threw herself, body and soul, into the project. And, as often happens, the more she did, the more opportunities came her way.

The first bit of self-made good luck came after she organized a flurry of newspaper, radio and television interviews to publicize the convoy and raise funds for the journey. She had just given an interview on the BBC's top-rated show *Good Morning with Anne and Nick* when the producers called her aside. They wanted two things. Could they make a program about the convoy? And did Heather want to become a guest presenter on the show? Hardly able to believe it, Heather said yes to both questions.

Away from the television studios Heather was getting noticed by an awful lot of other people as well. Reporter Kathryn Flett says, "I remember being at a social gathering of media types back in 1993 when the hostess announced that at the very last minute Heather Mills wouldn't be able to make it. 'Right,' I said. 'And who is Heather Mills?' 'You know. The model who lost her leg.' I was none the wiser. 'And quite possibly the most determined woman I have ever met,' my hostess concluded."

That determination was also being felt in Zagreb. Heather knew that the paperwork for her convoy needed to be perfect if it was to be allowed into the still war-torn country. And despite all her calls to the Ministry of Health, they were missing vital permits as her end of October deadline approached. Heather was terrified that bureaucracy might derail the most important journey of her life. So once more, she took charge personally. She rang the minister, Dr. Tonkovic, on a daily basis until they got the documents they needed. Then, exactly on schedule, the two fully loaded trucks began their journey across Europe. Everyone was about to find out if it had all been worthwhile.

The first problems began just 24 hours later. Heather and Bob had flown to Zagreb and were waiting for the trucks and television crew. The city was swamped with people after a recent Papal visit and nothing was going smoothly. Heather and Bob were refused access to the workshop where they were due to carry out the first fittings. It meant they couldn't start instructing the local doctors on how the parts all went together. Then, Heather got a call from the truck drivers. It seemed that, despite all their efforts with the paperwork, the border police were still refusing to let them through.

Heather remembers walking the streets of Zagreb overcome with quite uncharacteristic self-doubt. She was terrified that everything was going to go wrong. The first half dozen amputees were expecting to have their new limbs fitted the next day. Their hopes were so high. Their trust and their confidence would be shattered if they had to be turned away.

After calling everyone she could think of, Heather knew there was nothing else she could do but wait. And the next day, less than 12 hours late, the trucks did make it to their destination. The work could begin.

Three amputees were waiting patiently for their fittings that first day. Two of them were nineteen-years-olds. The third was a little girl of just eight. Heather remembers that all of them had a quiet dignity that brought tears to her eyes. Just as moving were the parents of eight-year-old Martine. She had lost her left leg to a landmine. Her parents had been told that it would be years before she was big enough to qualify for one of the few adult limbs available in the country. Her proud mom and dad were both were crying when the child-sized limb was made for their daughter. It wasn't easy. But after walking the length of the warehouse while holding Heather's hand, the girl was able to walk all the way back on her own. Heather was crying as she watched her. This tiny, brave child took her breath away. This was why they were all in Croatia.

One final incident is worth noting regarding those first few days fitting limbs in Zagreb. It happened when the team were working with the nineteen-year-old soldier, Sasha. Heather walked past him several times as he sat waiting for his fitting. She recognized a terrible sadness in his eyes. She guessed that he was feeling what she had once felt: that losing a limb meant giving up on all his dreams. She could tell how little this man of action wanted to be surrounded by the crippled and the maimed. Without speaking much of his language, she also sensed he felt patronized by the rich, perfect western Europeans who were trying to pick up the pieces of his life.

Instinctively, Heather knew what to do. She needed to show him that she, at least, wasn't perfect. She was wearing jeans, a long white coat and comfortable shoes. Clearly he had no idea that she too had lost a leg. Without thinking twice, she showed him. She took off her foot as she sat next to him and let him examine her stump. It was almost exactly the same as his. With Renata acting as an interpreter, she told the soldier that she too had given up hope for her future. But that her new leg had changed everything.

"Now I can ski, I can go running, I can rollerskate," she said. When Heather left him, Sasha was still looking sad. But he was also looking thoughtful. By the time he left the warehouse with his new leg, the doctors said he had started to smile.

Heather and everyone else were exhausted when their first five-day session ended. But they knew the good work would continue for many months after they had left. Teams of doctors from across the country had been watching and making notes as the first prosthetic limbs had been built and fitted. The 5,000 disassembled limb parts, plus several hundred wheelchairs and crutches, were now being sent out to hospitals and clinics around the country. Thousands of lives would change for the better.

The television documentary Heather had helped make had also been well-received. So much so that the producers tracked her down while she took a few days break in America, just after it was aired. They had set up the first "guest presenter" slot for her to film. But they needed it done fast.

"It's the day after tomorrow. And it's in London," they said.

"No problem. I'll be back. I'll see you then." Heather got a cab to the nearest airport and booked the first flight to London. She would never refuse paid work. She would never say no to a job. When she got back to her apartment, she was given more details of her task. She had to go to London's five-star Hyde Park Hotel to interview Keanu Reeves. The rollercoaster ride of her life was bringing as many surprises as ever.

Inside the hotel, Heather admits to a momentary lapse of confidence. All of the industry's most experienced interviewers seemed to be there. Wherever she looked she could see the faces she had watched on television for years. How would she cope amongst them? Did she really know what to do? As she took a seat, she got another shock. The running order for the interview session had her down as the first to question Keanu. She had hoped to be able to learn from the others before speaking. Now she wouldn't even be able to do that. If this had happened to her five years before, Heather admits she might have panicked. She might even have run from the room. But, in 1994, it was a much stronger lady who caught Keanu's eye. It was a lady who no longer feared anything.

"Yes, it was daunting, but I just took a deep breath and got on with it," she told fellow journalist Julie Cohen afterwards.

"My attitude to life is different now. I just felt that the worst thing is that I would be terrible and have to do it again. But as it turned out Keanu was charming and the piece was fine."

Heather was proving to be a breath of fresh air on television. Her accent was as strong as ever. Some viewers certainly hated it. But her enthusiasm was infectious. Reviewers said her overall attitude was perfect for daytime television. "She strikes you as someone you would like to have as a friend," said critic Andrew Douglas. "She doesn't over complicate things, she asks the kind of questions we would ask if we were in her position, and she always seems happy to laugh at herself if things go wrong. She looks great, which helps, but in a very real and natural way. She's tough, but she isn't intimidating. It's the perfect daytime television package and fewer people have it than you might think."

Getting noticed on television was opening other doors for Heather. She got a call asking if she had ever done any public speaking. She hadn't. But as usual she said she would happily give it a try. It was the right answer.

"The after-dinner speaking circuit can be extraordinarily lucrative for the right people, but not everyone does well on it," says Natasha Stevenson, who books big names for corporate, sales and celebratory events. "It is gladiatorial, and you need a lot of self-confidence to cope. For many events, you have to sit with your hosts throughout a long dinner, then stand up to speak when a lot of the other guests may have had too much to drink, might be feeling a bit bored and can be ready to heckle. If you buckle under the pressure, you won't be asked back."

Stevenson says you need two other key qualities: a sense of humor and a strong overall message. Heather had both. She made herself the butt of several jokes as she re-told anecdotes about her false leg falling off in fancy restaurants or setting off the alarms at airports. And she was inspirational when she detailed her own philosophy about survival.

"The final reason why Heather did so well in the public speaking world was because she so often surprised her hosts," says Stevenson. "A lot of them didn't expect much depth from a blond, former swimwear model. They expected a frivolous, lightweight speech about the celebrity lifestyle. Instead, they got some harrowing stories about land mine victims, amputees and beating the odds. This was what made Heather so successful."

What Heather also offered was professionalism. The people who booked her came to know she would always be on time, she would always look good, and she would always charm her hosts before and after the speeches. Little wonder that she was heavily in demand and could collect up to $20,000 for a speech.

"I do one a week. If I was greedy, I could do two a day," she said. Heather also liked the contacts she made during her corporate speeches. More convoys of disassembled limbs were still being organized for Croatia and she was constantly facing new logistical challenges. Sometimes the team might need leaflets printed. Sometimes they would need someone to pay for gas from their regular jobs. Sometimes they would simply want volunteers to be given time off to help out. Heather was shameless about calling in favors from the people she had met while giving speeches. She remembered how her dad had networked up at the theater in Newcastle. He had taught her well.

By the mid 1990s, Heather was also involved in several other charities. She was raising money for the Calvert Trust, a unique program offering getaways and personal challenges to disabled people and their families. She was also learning more about the effects landmines were having far beyond the Balkans. She carried on pushing for more news coverage of the issue and lobbied government officials to raise the subject in international meetings. She fully accepted that the more television work she did, the more useful her own name became. So she thought of setting up a foundation called "The Heather Mills Trust" to pool resources and co-ordinate relief efforts. What she didn't know was that this idea would one day be used against her.

With so much going on in her life, Heather admits she had started to take Raffaele for granted. They had been living together since she had left hospital. They still made a striking couple when they had the energy for a night out on the town. But Heather always knew their relationship had weak foundations. She couldn't forget that they had separated just before her accident. She feared that Raffaele might only have stayed at her side out of guilt. The pair parted on amicable terms in early 1995. It is worth noting that Raffaele—who consistently refuses to talk to the press—has never had a single bad word to say about his ex-girlfriend.

The newly single Heather threw herself back into her work. Her public speaking career had really taken off. International business groups wanted her to lead motivational events and she was now speaking across Europe and beyond. She considered becoming a life coach and started to write notes for a possible self-help book. Then, out of the blue, she fell in love.

The whirlwind romance began at the stunningly beautiful Hurlingham Club in West London. Every summer the club hosts an all-star tournament, which is both a key part of the warm-up to Wimbledon and a popular part of the "high society" scene. It certainly wasn't somewhere Heather could ever have imagined attending when she was knocking a ball around the battered tennis courts of Newcastle as a girl.

In 1995, the tournament organizer was 31-year-old Marcus Stapleton and he got to talking to Heather when he mingled among the VIP guests. The pair were instantly attracted to each other. They exchanged numbers and arranged to meet up for dinner in two days' time.

A week later, Heather and her new man were laughing over strawberries and champagne at Wimbledon, where they watched Pete Sampras beat British hopeful Tim Henman. In the years ahead, Heather would try to brush over her love affair with Marcus, failing to mention it at all in most accounts of her life. But in 1995, it was serious.

She told friends it was "love at first sight," and that Marcus was "the one." She even talked of engagements and an early wedding. She was convinced she had found someone she wanted to grow old with. Marcus was handsome and well connected, and they both enjoyed a fun summer in London. Friends say they certainly sparkled at dinner parties and picnics where they couldn't keep their hands off each other. But when it came to the crunch, neither of them felt ready to settle down. By the end of the year, she and Marcus had gone their separate ways and Heather was busy looking for new distractions.

She decided that travel would take her mind of things, so she booked a month-long trip to America. It was January and she started off in a cold and windy San Francisco where she joined all the other tourists on Alcatraz, on the trams and the piers. Then she rented a little Dodge van and headed up to Lake Tahoe where some friends had a chalet. She skied long days and loved every minute. And that was only the start. Back in the van, she headed further east to Salt Lake City where she skied some more. Then, she did the final long stretch to Aspen where two other friends ran a sushi bar. The trip re-confirmed Heather's sense that she could cope on her own.

"I don't really think about being disabled or abled," she said when friends asked how she might have coped in a snow drift. She told them she would have coped just as well or badly as anyone else might have done.

It was the same back in the workplace. Heather hated the victim culture that left too many disabled people feeling sorry for themselves and expecting society to subsidize their lifestyles. "The bottom line is: if you are positive enough and fun to be with, whatever disability you have, people will employ you and want you to be around. If you sit and moan your head off, then they won't."

Her own personal brand of tough love went further—she thought all welfare benefits like unemployment pay should be scrapped. "What is the point of sitting around all day feeling sorry for yourself? Even if you are disabled there is always work you could do to help the community. We're not tough enough," she declared.

In her softer moments, Heather did accept that not every disabled person had her inner confidence. That's why she was doing more one-on-one counseling in hospitals and rehabilitation clinics across the country. Many of the visits began when parents of a young accident victim wrote to her saying their son or daughter had lost all hope for the future. Heather's visits often rekindled that hope. Jane Baker, an occupational therapist who worked with accident victims at several hospitals in South London, saw the magic first hand.

"It wasn't just what Heather said to the patients that did the trick. It was her attitude and the way she looked. Every time I saw her I was amazed at how fresh and energetic she was. She always looked like a winner and this rubbed off on our patients and on their parents."

Brenda Saville, a respected technical instructor working with lower limb amputees at the Chapel Allerton Hospital in Leeds, agreed that having a role-model like Heather, who was "young, fit and elegant-looking," was immensely valuable to her patients' self-esteem.

Spending so much time in hospitals meant Heather was a perfect fit for a new television show being planned for early 1998. It was called *The General* and would follow the real-life stories of workers and patients at Southampton General Hospital on England's south coast. Heather was chosen to present the show and carry out most of its live interviews.

From the start, everyone knew it would be both grueling and emotionally draining. It was filmed five days a week and Heather was on site getting ready from 6:30 a.m. every morning. Nurses say that when the cameras stopped rolling, Heather often wandered around the wards for several more hours, chatting to and checking up on some of the patients she had met earlier in the day. The production team talked of stressful mornings and relaxed afternoons. Once the day's program finished, everyone on the crew got on well. But some of the hospital administrators came to dread Heather's appearance at their office doors. As the months passed, she became a powerful patient advocate, pushing for new funding and care reviews. Off the record, some of the consultants felt that it had been a mistake to pick someone like Heather to present *The General*. They had wanted an air-head presenter who would read her scripts and then go home. Heather was a whole lot harder to handle.

To their relief, if to no one else's, *The General* was ultimately cancelled after a nearly six-month run. Heather moved back to London. She was taken on as a guest investigator looking at problems faced by disabled travelers for the BBC show *Summer Holiday* and had a short term contract presenting an early morning current affairs show on Talk Radio. Both jobs were good fun and great experience. But they weren't exactly regular work. Heather was starting to worry about the hand-to-mouth nature of being a freelance television presenter. One part of her liked the thrill of never knowing what might be around the next corner. Another hated the fact that there always seemed to be too many bills to pay.

In the past when Heather had been unhappy with her personal life or her career, she had always managed to find solace in her charity work. But, in 1998, this too was dragging her down. A couple of years before, she had been thrilled when Princess Diana had been converted to the anti-landmine cause. She watched as the Princess brought the world's attention to the mines and tried to pull every string she knew to try and set up a meeting with her. She was convinced that with her experience of the issue and Diana's international star power they could finally persuade the world community to ban the bombs. But Heather's overtures had all come to nothing. She hadn't managed to meet the Princess before her death in August 1997.

In the months that followed, Heather sensed the media's reluctance to cover an issue they now associated squarely with the late Princess. Heather had no idea how to push the story forward. In the spring of 1998, when she tried to arrange press conferences and photoshoots for an anti-landmine charity, she was accused of "copying" Diana and "trying to replace her in the public's affections." Heather almost cried in frustration.

She got through this latest low patch by getting back into the hospitals and spending more time with amputees and other disabled patients. A psychiatrist, who once looked back on Heather's life, said her charity work is a textbook example of displacement activity. His theory was that Heather deals with her own pain by focusing entirely on relieving the pain of others. What he failed to understand is that the people who got the benefit of Heather's experience couldn't care less why she was there. To them, all that mattered was that she made the effort.

"For me, Heather has rewritten what the words 'good Samaritan' mean," says her friend Bob Watts. "She will not just cross the road if she sees someone in trouble, she will start shouting to other people, 'Look, this person needs help,' and she will make sure they get it."

She has also proven to be a lot more than just a fair-weather friend. She is still in touch with many of the patients she first met in various hospitals many years ago. Something inside of Heather means she always goes the extra mile for those she thinks need the most help. In 1998, she proved it when she quietly gave her house keys to a heroin addict named Melissa.

CHAPTER NINE

The Real Heather Mills

It began on television. But this particular act of charity was never supposed to be for public consumption. Heather had been asked to go back on to her old daytime television show, *This Morning with Richard and Judy*, to talk about one of her closest new friends. The friend was Helen Smith, a young biochemistry student and talented pianist, who had lost her arm, her hand and both legs to meningitis. When they first met, Helen was struggling to get by with some of the least suitable limb replacements Heather had ever seen. Instead of a replacement hand, for example, the pretty young girl had been given the kind of ugly metal claw that looked like a throwback to another age.

Heather's very public outrage had persuaded a private individual to provide the funds for Helen to get state of the art replacement limbs from Bob Watts. The friends had been asked to appear on *This Morning* to show what a little extra cash could do, and also to start a campaign for more public funds for amputees. After their interview, Heather stayed on set to cover part of the regular "Dear Abby" style slot. The producers remember her for displaying typical northern bluntness with the callers. She refused to let anyone wallow in self-pity. Instead, she offered simple, practical solutions to their problems. It was yet more tough love, Heather Mills style.

The following week, Heather was asked back to dish out another dose of advice. As she sat having her hair and makeup done for her spot, Heather chatted to a middle-aged couple who were due to be interviewed just before her. Their 18-year-old daughter, Melissa Meredith, had disappeared. Apparently, she had begun smoking marijuana five years earlier and had gone downhill ever since. Her last known boyfriend was a heroin addict, and she had been sent to prison after being caught stealing to feed their drug habits. Her parents hadn't heard a word from her since her release. They were desperate.

Heather couldn't get the parents' story out of her mind when it was her turn to go on set. As a former teenage runaway herself, she knew how hard it was to make the first move when you want to go home. So she ignored her script and made a direct appeal to the couple's daughter. "Melissa, if you're watching, your parents love you," she said. She gave the station's phone number and begged the teenager to call. To everyone's amazement, Melissa did just that. She asked to speak to Heather.

Off camera and in private, Heather tried to give her the confidence to break free from her current circumstances. Then, on a whim, she made a promise. She wanted Melissa to go cold turkey in her parents' house. Then she could move in with her for as long as it took till she was fully on her feet again. It was an unconventional and potentially dangerous strategy. But Heather couldn't care less. She felt she recognized some kindred spirit in this frightened, lost girl. And it turned out that she was right.

Melissa did get clean after moving back to her childhood home. Then, she turned up at Heather's door.

Unable to decide where she wanted to live, Heather was renting a converted barn in the middle of the countryside just southwest of London. She had bought a dog, Oliver, and was enjoying a life of relative isolation. Neither she nor Melissa knew if this latest experiment would destroy the rural idyll—not least because, despite many phone conversations, this was the first time the pair had ever actually met.

Heather admits that the next few weeks and months were not all easy. She retains her zero tolerance approach to drugs, so she wouldn't accept any weakening of Melissa's resolve.

What she also did—and unashamedly so—was put Melissa to work. It began with chores around the barn. Then she asked Melissa to help do some of the administration work for her charity efforts. Finally, she made some calls and found an opening for Melissa at one of the Calvert Trust holiday centers that she supported. Again, it was all a gamble and could have gone wrong. But it didn't. Melissa thrived.

"Really what I tend to think works is to put people in situations where they are surrounded by people worse off than themselves and where they have got to take some sort of responsibility," Heather said later when she explained her recovery strategy. "With Melissa, I pretty much kept her off drugs by putting her to work with disabled kids." It was both that simple, and that hard.

Reporter Jasper Gerard was one of many who said this kind of transformation was possible only because of the strength of Heather's extraordinary personality. He had been asked to examine some of the claims Heather had made about her childhood and charitable work—part of what would be an ongoing campaign by newspaper bosses to prove she was an unreliable witness. But after spending a lot of time with her, Gerard came down quite squarely on Heather's side.

"Yes, you begin to wonder if all this is fantasy," he said after hearing a list of the various challenges she had overcome. "But even if it is, you are forced to concede that she will probably make it true. She is too remorseless to be denied."

He also noted how energetic she was. A part of her was clearly on permanent alert against showing any sign of weakness. Had she not had the accident, she is happy to admit that she might have slowed down or stopped taking on so many challenges. But as an amputee, Heather always felt she had something to prove. If there was even a hint that her disability meant she couldn't achieve any goal, then she wouldn't rest until she had proven the doubters wrong. She had already ticked sport, modeling and television presenting off her mental checklist. Now she decided to give up the barn in the country and add property development to the list.

In October 1997, she had spent $550,000 on an empty shell of a building just off Shaftsbury Avenue in the heart of London's theatreland. It was part of a huge derelict building that had previously been used as offices. It had no gas, no water and no internal walls. It would be an extreme makeover nearly a decade before the same name ABC series had even been thought of. In typical fashion, Heather decided to run the project on her own. It didn't go well. One of her plumbers started stalking her, one of her carpenters tried to move in, and all her builders walked out when they got a better offer from a nearby hotel group. Turning the empty space into a flashy London home ultimately cost double her original refurbishment budget and left her exhausted as well as broke.

But at least she had a fantastic place for parties. There were no neighbors nearby to disturb so the music could be played as loud as they liked. Up to sixty people could fit into the apartment and Heather prepared herself for a fantastic few years in the heart of the city. But then something strange happened. She realized that she wasn't a city girl after all. She and Oliver both missed the country. The apartment didn't suit either of them— even though Heather had designed every element of it herself.

"I thought that because it is in Soho, I should do the place in a minimalist style, but actually I like cosiness and clutter," she told a real estate agent when she asked how easy it would be to sell. He told her he could get a buyer within a week. The hidden lighting, steel door frames, mini-radiators and coloured glass bricks made the place a perfect bachelor pad, Heather was told.

"City bankers will love the huge shower as well," the real estate agent said.

"That was designed for me. I wanted room for a chair so I can perch my bum on it when I haven't got my leg on,'" she replied with typical honesty. She was equally unembarrassed when the agent opened the big wardrobes in the main bedroom and saw her spare leg propped up in the corner. "It's my falsie!" she told him as they both fell off their chairs laughing.

The reality of Heather's life popped up in other circumstances as well. A fellow guest remembers a tense incident when she sat down at a London dinner party that year. "We've met before," said the man opposite Heather as everyone did their introductions.

"We have? I'm afraid I don't remember," Heather said, clearly trying not to seem rude.

"Yes, I've seen you naked," the stranger said, as the whole room turned to look.

Her friend remembers Heather's anguished look at the man's wife, sitting next to him. No one could work out why the man was embarrassing everyone like this. Then he explained it. "I was the doctor on call after your accident. I was in the hospital. I was asked to get the death certificate because they thought you weren't going to live." Heather remembers being uncharacteristically stumped for words.

One thing was eating away at Heather as she approached the fifth anniversary of her accident. She had done several newspaper photoshoots over the years and had even taken part in the occasional charity fashion show. But her mainstream modeling work had dried up. In ordinary circumstances, she might have simply moved on to other things. But she couldn't stop thinking that her disability was a turnoff to casting directors. And she wanted to prove that this was wrong.

In the past, being a model had been a means to an end to Heather. It had been the easiest way a pretty young girl with precious few academic qualifications could make a decent living. Now, like so many other things in her life, it became a mission. She wanted to prove that losing a leg didn't make her undesirable or unemployable. That's what she had recently told nineteen-year-old hopeful model Candice Ward who she had counseled in the hospital after the girl had lost her right leg in a car accident. But was it true?

Heather started calling agents again and put the word out that she was ready for work. Nobody called. She had a new set of photographs taken to market herself. Still nothing. She went direct to some of the fashion bosses she had met on speaking engagements to see if they needed a new "face" for their campaigns. Still everyone said no.

Sitting at home, Heather knew she could just give in gracefully. But she also knew giving in wasn't in her nature. She was only 30 years old. She was as fit as she had ever been. She ate well, didn't smoke or take drugs and hardly drank any alcohol. She knew she looked good enough to work. She decided to cast her net even wider. She tried some of the overseas contacts she had made over the years, calling photographers, magazine editors and advertising agents. One of them, a marketing consultant and photographer named Marco Tricomi, came up trumps. He was working with the Italian cosmetics company Pascal on a campaign to launch a new range of waterproof makeup. The idea behind the campaign was to feature modern, active women who lived life to the fullest and didn't want to waste time worrying about their makeup. It was a role Heather felt she had been born to play. Marco agreed. He said he was due to be in London the next day and suggested a meeting. The pair bonded straight way.

"I will get you this contract," he remembers telling Heather—fully aware that she didn't quite believe him. While they had been talking she had told him of all the other promises she had been made in the past. All of which had come to nothing. He flew home and rang her the next day.

"Heather, they want to see you in Italy." Four days later, she was on a plane to meet the chairman of Pascal. She did a test shoot in Italy and the company loved it. Heather was back in business. The campaign itself was hugely energizing. In the first set of advertisements, she was filmed boxing, horseback riding and working-out before taking a dip in a spa bath—all, of course, with perfect makeup. In the second set of pictures, Heather felt even better. She was photographed lounging by the pool in a sexy evening gown. Her disability was totally forgotten.

"I'm the living proof that anything two legs can do, I can do better," she said, jubilantly, as news of the campaign broke. As usual, she was also ready for some typically shameless self-promotion. She did nothing to stop the rumors that she was collecting $1.5 million for the job. In reality, this was standard bravado. Analysts say the figure could just about have been the amount the entire campaign was costing. Heather's share, while large, was only a fraction of the total and much of it would be swallowed up in expenses, fees and taxes. But at least it kept her solvent.

"I've spent four years working mainly for other people's benefit. Now I'm doing something for me," she told friends back in London. By the late 1990s, she was either the unpaid patron or the primary figurehead of 11 different charities and had links with many more. Some weeks, she spent as many as four days counseling and working on projects for her favored causes. All of this was only possible if she carried on winning the occasional high profile and well paid job.

What she found when she got back from Italy was that these jobs often seemed to come in batches. When one client wanted her then everyone seemed to want her. In many ways it was the same kind of feast or famine existence that her father had led back in Washington. But in her case, Heather was pleased to say things never got so bad that her furniture was taken away by the bailiffs.

The next fun job she had was to make a holiday program back in Croatia. She could hardly have asked for anything nicer. But bearing in mind how well she knew the country, she admits she should have packed a little better. Most of the filming was done in Dubrovnik and Heather walked around the immense town walls, up and down hundreds of steps, round cobbled alleys and across shiny marble squares—all in ridiculously high heels.

"I don't have much choice. I've only got my high-heeled leg with me so I can't stick on a pair of trainers," she told the crew with a smile. The following month she won more regular work as a presenter on a new campaigning show called *That's Esther*. The veteran reporter Esther Rantzen was the main host, while Heather focused on disabled and underprivileged people in Britain and around the world. Her role was to fight in their corner against injustices or discrimination, and she did it doggedly. The early ratings weren't great, but television reviewers loved Heather's performance. One paper called her "the one-legged wonder-girl," which she was happy to take as a compliment.

All things considered, Heather's life was looking particularly good as winter turned to spring in 1999. It was about to get a lot better. She was going to go through another of her little-known whirlwind romances. Within weeks she was going to be engaged. If she hadn't also met a certain ex-Beatle, she would have been married by the late summer of 1999.

CHAPTER TEN
Chris versus Paul

Heather's love life had been in the doldrums since she had split from Marcus Stapleton nearly four years earlier. Friends had set her up on the occasional date and she certainly met plenty of eligible men at her speaking engagements and charity functions. But she had become cynical. She saw men as distractions and didn't want to repeat any of the mistakes she felt she had made in the past. Her comments on the subject have been harsh in the extreme. "I look back on my life before the accident and I ask myself: 'Why didn't I achieve as much then as I am now?' The answer is simple—I was putting too much of my energies into relationships with men. But, frankly, most of them just aren't worth the effort. You spend 20 years with a man and what have you got at the end of it? Nothing. I have extremely high standards and expectations. I suppose I'm being selfish, but I can't be bothered to waste energy pandering to men who are, so many of them, little boys," was how she described her feelings to friends.

It was tough stuff. But Heather was speaking from bitter experience. "I can't find a man confident enough to take me on. They either want to compete with me or lock me in the house and put me in an apron," she told a newspaper reporter who asked about her relationships in early 1999.

But a different reporter remembers a much softer Heather Mills who had clearly not lost her romantic side. Frances Hardy, who was writing a profile for the *Daily Mail* newspaper, remembers Heather's voice falling almost to a whisper as she spoke of her hopes for the future. "I would dearly love to have a child," Heather told her. "But only if I found that ideal man. I would never have a child as a single woman because that would be selfish." Frances remembers something else Heather told her. "I'm going back to the old fashioned ways," she had said with a laugh. "I want to go on dates, be courted and sent flowers."

Heather created quite a stir on May 20, 1999 when she was asked to name one of the winners of the "Pride of Britain Awards" at London's Dorchester Hotel. The bravery award went to one of her old friends, Helen Smith, who then attempted to make a speech to the room. Unfortunately, no one could hear her. The only microphone on the stage was attached at head height to a lectern. Helen was in a wheelchair. As the event organizers tried to work out what to do, Heather strode forward to take direct action. She grabbed the microphone, ripped it out of the lectern and handed it to Helen. Some 500 guests in the ballroom began a spontaneous round of applause. Once more, Heather had made her mark.

"The Pride of Britain Awards" were the brainchild of Piers Morgan, the then editor of Britain's *Daily Mirror* newspaper, now a judge on *America's Got Talent.* He had wanted a forum to recognize the country's unsung heroes and heroines: the people who overcome adversity every day, in private, and with no reward. The event was increasingly star-studded. In 1999, the key guests included the likes of Tony and Cherie Blair, Queen Noor of Jordan, Richard Branson and, of course, Sir Paul McCartney.

Years later, in his best-selling book *The Insider*, Piers wrote of the "fantastic, rousing speech" 31-year-old Heather made after presenting Helen with her award. Piers also wrote of Paul's reaction to the speech. "I like the way she talks, she's a gutsy girl," Paul said when Piers discussed her charity work. And Piers said he himself noticed Heather's "striking resemblance" to Paul's late wife Linda—not just physically, but in the "strong-willed and independent" way she spoke. He suggested that Paul contact her to see if he could help one of her charities. "Yes, might just do that," he replied. Wheels were in motion—but things were about to get very complicated. Two days after the awards ceremony, Heather flew to the Far East to film her latest *That's Esther* show. She was about to have her next whirlwind romance. By the time she came back to Britain, she would be in love and engaged to be married. If Paul really fancied her, he would have to get in line.

Heather's new fiancé was television director Chris Terrill. He was sixteen years older than her, and heading the crew for the *That's Esther* show Heather was shooting in Cambodia. It was her highest profile trip to date. The idea was to promote the work of the Voluntary Service Overseas charity—a sort of British Peace Corps. The charity's ambassador was the Duchess of Kent, who was traveling with the team to explain some of the charity's work to Heather. For her part, the Duchess remembers how relaxed Heather was with the maimed and disabled children they met— and how easily she inspired them with hope for the future.

"I remember standing back and watching her," the Duchess said later. "There were about thirty to forty children and they were all limbless, and she was so gentle with them. But also she has a wonderful sense of humor, and they were laughing with her. I was just amazed by her." The Duchess says she could sense how well Heather led by example. The children could see that she had coped after losing a leg. She gave them the inspiration to follow suit.

Chris admits to being just as captivated by Heather. They had met little more than two weeks prior to the Cambodian trip, and their first serious conversations about prison rehabilitation and drug offenders were soon broken up by peals of laughter. Their senses of humor clicked. He wanted to know more about her, and they talked long into the nights once they arrived in Cambodia. Looking back, it was all too much, too soon. But the resolutely single Chris was convinced that Heather was the woman he had spent a lifetime seeking. Out of nowhere, he decided he wanted to marry her. So he proposed to her on that very first business trip. They were in a fishing boat drifting up the Mekong river on their way to the incredible Angkor Wat when he spoke. They had known each other for less than a month. Equally overcome and optimistic, Heather said "yes" with barely a second thought. When they got back to dry land, they bought a ring. It was a bamboo hoop from a local market, which cost the equivalent of a quarter. In every photograph taken of the couple on the trip they are arm in arm and smiling from ear-to-ear.

"Hi, Heather. It's Paul McCartney here. Would you give me a ring?"

That was one of the messages Heather found on her answering machine when she came back from Cambodia. She was a newly engaged woman. She decided it must be a joke. After seeing Paul at the Pride of Britain Awards, she had told one of her friends how young and handsome he had looked. *Someone's pulling my leg*, she thought. So she deleted the message and got on with her day. The following evening she got back to her flat and there was a second message.

"Hi, Heather. It's Paul McCartney again." Once more he said he wanted her to call him. As she sat down, Heather felt herself blush. Had she snubbed one of the most famous men in Britain? She composed herself and rang the number he had left, still convinced it would be a dead line, a Chinese restaurant or some other place her friends would find amusing. It wasn't.

Sir Paul's secretary confirmed he had been trying to get in touch with her and would call again very soon. Heather put the phone down feeling surprisingly nervous. It wasn't that she was star-struck—she had just come back from a trip with a member of the royal family, after all. Nor was it that she was a particular fan of the Beatles or Paul's solo work. She liked "Here Comes the Sun," but years later she would admit she knew very few of Paul's albums and had only heard of one of the Beatles' films. So what was it that was making her feel so jumpy? At the time, Heather didn't know. But she did hope he would call back.

As fate would have it, Chris answered the phone when Paul next rang. He and Heather were curled up on her sofa getting ready to watch their episode of *That's Esther*. He handed the phone over to his fiancé, pretty impressed at the kind of company she kept. Chris was also impressed by the way she handled the call. There was no obsequious groveling from Heather. She might be talking to the most famous man in British music, but it seemed that Sir Paul would have to wait his turn. Heather told him she was busy. She said he should switch his television on and to ring back when the program was over.

Half an hour later, he did just that. Heather and Paul had their first proper conversation, with Chris listening in on her side of it from the sofa. Heather, in particular, was in business mode. It seemed that Paul was interested in the landmines issue and had been doing some research into how a new generation of false limbs could help amputees rebuild their lives. Heather was in her element. She loved bouncing ideas around about the best ways to tackle these problems. And she had recently learned of a terrible new crisis that was unfolding in Sierra Leone.

Over there, the problem wasn't just the landmines. It was the brutality of the rebel soldiers who hacked the arms off children in revenge attacks on their parents. This hidden war was creating a new generation of upper arm amputees who faced entirely different challenges than those faced by those who lost their legs. Heather had spent much of the past few months unsuccessfully trying to raise awareness of this unfolding tragedy. She was thrilled at the prospect of converting someone like Paul to her cause. His influence could save lives and she could hardly get the words out fast enough as she rattled through statistics showing the scale of the problem.

With Chris looking on, she suddenly wondered if she had been talking too much. This probably wasn't the reaction Paul normally got when he called people for a quick chat. Had she scared him off? Heather remembers a pause on the line before she got the answer. "Well, let's meet up to talk about it," he said.

After comparing schedules, Heather and Paul agreed to meet in his London office in just over a week's time. In the intervening days, Heather had a wedding to plan. She and Chris had decided they wanted to be married in the summer and it took a while to find a venue that wasn't already booked. They shared very specific ideas about their big day. They wanted a simple official ceremony at the Registry Office and then a big non-religious "humanist" celebration with all their friends and families.

The problem was that both of them knew they had a lot of bridge-building to do if they were to get their friends and family onboard. Heather's friends were particularly upset that she had suddenly gotten engaged to someone they hadn't even met. Fiona, still working in Greece, was particularly adamant that she wanted to check the man out before giving her approval for the match. If anything, things were even harder for Chris. His friends were equally dumfounded that their 47-year-old bachelor friend was going to be married within months. His family was distraught. Years later, he said his parents had organized "crisis meetings" about his engagement—even before they had met his fiancé.

When he did take Heather round for dinner, he says things got worse. His parents put on a brave face, he said. "But they knew instinctively that she was wrong for me." But the romance of their Cambodian nights took a while to fade. Heather and Chris were still happy. They booked both of their marriage ceremonies, sent out the invitations and even agreed to let a glossy magazine photograph the event for them. Heather's rollercoaster life was moving faster than ever.

Heather checked her look in every shop window she passed as she walked to her first private meeting with Sir Paul. She couldn't figure out why she was so nervous. But she was. This meeting mattered and she wanted to look good. *Be professional, be businesslike, be ready.* That's what she was telling herself. She wanted Sir Paul to like her ideas. But something deep inside was already telling her that she wanted him to like her as well.

He was a grieving widower and an international icon. She wanted to impress him. She wanted to make him smile.

The office itself was totally anonymous and surprisingly modest. No flash marble halls, no secretaries or assistants scurrying around and catering to their master's every whim. Just one charming receptionist who smiled, said Heather was expected and that Sir Paul would be with her shortly.

She sat in one of the two leather chairs and tried to stay composed. She positioned her legs so she could stand up smoothly when required. *I'm not going to let him see me stumble*, she vowed. And when she saw him she knew she would have to move fast to keep up with him. He practically bounded around the corner and across the reception area to shake her hand—all very businesslike and correct. *He's like a teenager*, she thought as he guided her to his own office. A charming one, she added as he stood aside so she could enter first. *I like him.*

The crisis in Sierra Leone dominated the conversation. She told him about the joint relief effort she was planning with a fellow charity worker named Edward Pennington-Ridge. Ed had worked out that low cost false limbs could be made in many third world countries using things like wood and rubber that would otherwise go to waste. Another charity, World Hope International Clinic, was already in Sierra Leone and Heather was desperately trying to co-ordinate everyone's efforts so no time, money or expertise would be wasted. Paul said he was looking to fund new charitable concerns. So, once more Heather found herself talking at a thousand miles an hour. She wanted to persuade him that her cause deserved his support. She liked his concise, professional approach to the subject. He listened to her presentation, then asked half a dozen questions. He wanted a proper written proposal of what she thought she could do and how much it would cost. Once she had drawn up a detailed business plan, he said they should meet again to discuss it. That was it. They shook hands and Heather headed home to work on the proposal.

Later she said two other details struck her from the meeting. The first was how energetic Paul was. She knew, of course, that he had been a passionate animal rights activist alongside his former wife, Linda. She hoped some of this conviction could be brought to her own cause. The second detail that struck her was the final look on his face as she walked into the elevator and left his office.

He's checking me out, she thought to herself in astonishment.

"Yes, I was," Paul admitted later when he was asked about his memories of that day.

More seriously, Heather had some tough decisions to make as she put the business plan together for Paul. She didn't know how much money he was planning to give. But she was hoping it would be ten, twenty or even thirty thousand pounds. So what would she actually do with his check? Today she admits that the Heather Mills Health Trust was simply a grand name for her own personal endeavours. When she needed to go to the Balkans or anywhere else to help oversee any of her relief efforts she simply paid her own way. Over the years she thought she had probably spent a huge proportion of her income on her good causes. Because she had never set herself up as a properly registered charity or foundation, no one had ever examined her books. But she knew she couldn't have a lump sum from Paul sitting in her personal bank account. So when she wasn't organizing her wedding, working on her television show, counseling her group of hospital patients and writing up her Sierra Leone business plan, she knew she would have to formally register her charity. This was the exact moment that she became seriously ill.

No one on the set of *That's Esther* knew that Heather had suffered a cancer scare just before leaving for Cambodia. Doctors had spotted some suspicious growths on her cervix and she had rushed in to the hospital to have them removed. The immediate prognosis was good. It seemed they had spotted the problem in time and dealt with it in full. Heather was booked for check-ups every six-months and was told to slow down for the rest of the year. Her doctor was a friend of hers. He didn't think even for a moment that she would follow the last part of his orders.

Heather was in the television studio when she started to feel ill. It seemed that her immune system had been weakened by the operation and she had contracted dengue fever in Cambodia. The symptoms kicked in immediately. For nearly a week Heather was overcome with exhaustion, unable to eat or drink, and her whole body was wracked with pain. When she was cold, she shivered so much she thought her bed might collapse. Minutes later, she would find herself sweating so much she could practically wring out her sheets. She had canceled her next meeting with Paul and as soon as she felt well enough to leave her bed Heather knew she had to cancel something else as well. She knew, suddenly, that she didn't want to go through with her wedding.

Heather is clearly not the kind of person to let other people tell her what to do. But, in her heart of hearts, she admits that Chris's family was making an effort to push her away. Their first meeting had been tough. Afterwards, in the cold light of day, Heather started to wonder if they might be right. Wasn't she just a little too old to think a vacation romance would last a lifetime?

As usual, Heather turned to her sister Fiona for advice. They talked over the phone for hours at a time as they analyzed what they thought it took to make a relationship work. One thing they agreed upon was that you needed enough time to truly know the other person. Heather thought back ruefully to her earlier desire to "go on dates, be courted and sent flowers." She had known then that a lengthy, traditional courtship was a good idea. How had she allowed herself to forget?

That summer, less than two weeks before her wedding day, Heather plucked up her courage and did what she felt she had to do. She told Chris that she couldn't go through with the ceremony. His parents were right. They would be better off apart.

Looking back it was all an extraordinary episode in Heather's life. It is one she has hardly ever discussed in public. In private she told friends the engagement was like a "moment of madness." It was as if the woman who barely touched alcohol had become drunk on emotion and optimism. Canceling the deal with the magazine, returning her wedding gifts, and spending what should have been her big day alone was hugely humiliating. She knew their friends were talking non-stop about various bizarre theories about why the wedding hadn't taken place. Heather refused to confirm or deny any of them. She was just pleased that she had sobered up in time.

Throwing herself into her work helped Heather cope with the strains in her private life—just as it always had. Against all odds, she enjoyed making the Heather Mills Health Trust an official charity. The process was far simpler than she had imagined. With hindsight she knew she should have done it years ago. But with hindsight she might have done many things differently in her life. She is a big believer in the fact that we have to face the situation we are in now, not the situation we would like to be in. And that we should focus on the future, rather than dwelling on the past.

In July of 1999, Heather had two more meetings with Paul as they ironed out more details of the work they planned to do in Sierra Leone. By the end of the second meeting, Heather was still refusing to believe that there was anything more than a friendly twinkle in Paul's eye. "I thought he was very cute, but it didn't enter my head that he fancied me," she said later. Not everyone agreed. Ever since first hearing about the phone calls and the meetings, Fiona had thought that Paul might have an ulterior motive for getting in touch. By the time she told Heather of her suspicions, it seemed as if she might be right. And none other than Richard Branson would confirm it. Heather had a fundraising meeting with the tycoon immediately after seeing Paul. She was so pleased with their progress that she told him about it.

"He fancies you," Richard said. "Don't forget I was sitting next to him at the *Mirror* awards."

If it was true, then Heather was genuinely flattered. But she had no great desire to explore what might happen next. After the debacle with Chris, she told friends she had resigned herself to being single for many more years. "My walls are very high now," she said as she effectively put her personal life on hold. That said, Heather was very aware of how useful Paul could be to her charitable causes. She knew that people listened when he spoke and she was desperate to share his spotlight. But would he really turn it on to her and her new campaign in Sierra Leone?

The days passed and still no check came through. In the early hours of the morning, Heather felt herself panic at the thought that Paul might never get around to writing it. If so, she knew she would find the money another way. She always had. But when children were being maimed and injured on a daily basis, she knew time was of the essence.

Paul didn't let Heather down. He gave her a sealed envelope containing the check at their fourth meeting. Heather opened it the moment she got into her taxi for the ride home. She couldn't believe it. It was for £150,000, roughly the equivalent of $300,000. The Heather Mills Health Trust could now do more good than she had ever imagined possible. Heather then made four phone calls. She called Paul to thank him. She called one of her charity's new trustees, Trudi, to say they were really in business. She called Ed to say the Sierra Leone project had gotten the green light. And she called Fiona to say that she really liked Paul McCartney. Fiona had the good grace not to say she had known it all along.

As he was her biggest single donor, Heather kept Paul fully up to date with the work she was doing. They spoke on the phone. They had another business meeting. Then they went to dinner. Something was clearly afoot.

What Heather didn't do at any stage was open up completely about her private life. The woman who has been endlessly accused of exaggerating her past and over-emphasizing her achievements decided to be a lot more restrained when talking to Paul about her past relationships. In fact, she airbrushed her former fiancé out of her history in just seven words. "I've just split up with my boyfriend," was all she told Paul at their first dinner. It was perhaps the under-statement of the year. But Heather hadn't wanted the truth to turn Paul away.

The couple went to a vegetarian restaurant near Harrods department store in Knightsbridge. Heather loved how relaxed Paul was with the staff—who he clearly knew well. She remembered how passionate he and Linda had been about animal rights and food standards. He told her how important it was to have a healthy diet. She told him how healthy eating and wheatgrass from the health clinic in Florida had changed her life six years earlier. Something else struck her: she felt she saw a kindred spirit in his eyes when he talked about his favorite causes. She told Fiona that the sadness seemed to disappear when he let rip about the things he believed in. Heather also told Fiona about the kiss at the end of the evening. It was a full-on kiss on the lips, which left her lurching sideways having expected a simple peck on the cheek. If she hadn't long since learned to be steady on her feet she might have ended up on the floor.

"We should meet up again," Paul said when she had recovered and climbed into her taxi. So they did. In private, several times a week for the next three months.

What was immediately clear to Heather was that this slow-burn relationship would face none of the external pressures that had driven her and Chris apart. The few friends and family members who knew about it couldn't have been more supportive. Fiona and Paul clicked instantly when they met, and she found an equally strong friend in one of his close confidantes. Paul had presented an award at the Pride of Britain gala to a very dear friend of his and Linda's. She was Juliet Gellatley, the founder of VIVA, the Vegetarian International Voice for Animals. She would soon become an equally close friend of Heather's.

"I instinctively liked her on our first meeting. I immediately recognized in her the unmistakable attributes of an experienced campaigner—passionate, dedicated, unbelievably energetic and caring. Endlessly caring," Juliet said after meeting Paul's new partner.

Not, of course, that either she or Paul were using the word partner at this stage. He still hadn't gotten over Linda's death from cancer less than two years earlier. Heather had just canceled her wedding. Both wanted to tread carefully. What both of them enjoyed was the chance to be romantic. Heather was certainly getting the dates and the courting she had dreamed of. And when she got flowers from him, they meant far more than an expensive bunch delivered from a florist. One day, Paul might hand her a wildflower he had picked on his estate in Sussex. The next day, he might give her a shiny leaf, a sprig of rosemary, a chestnut or a feather.

"I always had this dream of a knight in shining armor," Heather said about those idyllic early days. "Someone who was romantic. I never went for guys with money, I just wanted romance. He is the most romantic guy I have ever met."

A side-effect of their joint desire to stay out of the public eye meant they got to know each other very well, very quickly. Apart from Fiona and Juliet, they rarely spent time with other people. Nor did they go out to the theater or even to see a film. Instead, they spent hours talking as they walked around Paul's country estate, normally with Oliver racing around at their side. They went on long drives together and watched autumn sunsets over England's south coast. Heather cooked meals in a friend's London apartment while Paul returned the favor in the country. It was all absolutely perfect.

Heather remembers the exact moment she realized she was in love with Paul. She and Fiona were on vacation in Florida while Paul was in America on business. He said he would come over to their hotel to say hello. "I'll see you on the beach. I'll be in my boat," he said as he hung up the phone. Heather and Fiona agreed it sounded wildly exciting. They imaged the huge floating gin palaces that got moored in harbors like Monte Carlo and Miami and Heather prepared herself for a little bit of rock and roll excess. She didn't get it. As she lay reading her book in the sun, Paul paddled up in a tiny little dinghy. That was his boat.

Heather climbed aboard with a huge smile on her face. She had never felt more relaxed or comfortable in anyone's company. Paul always surprised her and always made her laugh. Most of the time, she felt he was more like a little boy than an award-winning music legend. She was convinced he was the man for her.

Back in Britain, Paul was clearly just as interested. While he was spending Christmas with his family as usual, he certainly didn't want Heather to feel miserable without him. So on December 23rd, he cut down a Christmas tree on his country estate, drove it over to Heather's house, and set it up in her garden. On Christmas Eve, they decorated it together before he headed off to join his family. Heather sat in her kitchen that night looking out at the lights twinkling on her tree. She might not have Paul in person. But he was certainly there in spirit.

Heather's friends could all tell that something good was happening in her life—but they would have to wait a while longer to find out what it was. Bob Watts was one of them. "When Heather is with someone special her face lights up. It just changes. She had that look when I met her recently. I knew she was in love but not who with," he said that Christmastime. Bob, more than most, had seen Heather through plenty of highs and lows since fitting her first false limb. He was thrilled that she seemed to be firmly on the up again. Immediately after decorating the tree, Paul had given Heather another wonderful surprise. As soon as Christmas was out of the way, he wanted to introduce her to his family. It was official proof of how serious they had become. In the years ahead, there would be endless speculation over whether Paul's daughter, Stella, in particular, did or didn't like Heather. But their first meeting on New Year's Eve of 1999 went like a dream.

Just before the event, Heather told Fiona that she was terrified on several different levels. Her biggest worry was that she would seem to be replacing Linda. The fact that Paul's children were all adults wasn't going to make this any easier. Her other worry was more general. The more Paul told her about the McCartney family's New Year parties, the more overwhelming they seemed. It was a true gathering of the clan. Everyone descended upon Liverpool from all points of the compass and threw themselves into a long-established routine of house parties, meals, games and drinks. Heather was terrified that she would forget people's names or would be made to feel like an outsider. She needn't have worried for a moment.

The McCartney family was as different from her family as it was possible to be. They were warm, noisy, tactile and demonstrative. She says she lost count of the number of hugs and kisses she enjoyed as everyone prepared to party. She also loved the multi-generational nature of the celebration. Having always lived hundreds of miles from her own grandparents, she envied those who had a much closer relationship. But for all these differences, Heather did find one easy connection with the McCartneys. They were all typical Liverpool people—classic down-to-earth people Brits call "scousers" who reminded her enormously of the equally gregarious people from her native Newcastle, known as "geordies." She felt at home in their company and had the best New Year's Eve of her life.

The other big story was that this was no ordinary New Year's Eve. The following morning was the start of the new millennium. The whole world felt fresh and exciting again. Heather and Paul were in for the adventure of their lives.

CHAPTER ELEVEN

Going Public

Heather's year began with an incredible birthday surprise. She would be 32 on the 12th of January, but had resigned herself to spending the day without Paul. Straight after the millennium celebrations he had flown off for a winter getaway in the Caribbean with his children. Heather hadn't wanted to intrude. Paul had other ideas. He wanted to spend ten days of quality time with his family. But then he asked Heather to fly out and join the party. Everyone could have some fun in the sun together. Then his children would head home, and he and Heather could be alone in paradise for her birthday.

Heather jumped at the chance—and found out that when Paul said paradise that was exactly what he meant. They were booked into a villa on the beach at Parrot Cay, one of the most exclusive of the Turks and Caicos islands. They went swimming, sailing, snorkelling and even scuba diving. Heather discovered that Paul's romantic side certainly traveled well. One day, he painted their names on a stone on the beach. The next day, he organized a candle-lit dinner on a table next to the waves. In between, they lay in the sun, talked about anything and everything, and felt entirely comfortable together. Heather told friends that after eight months she felt as if she knew Paul better than some people she had known for eight years. Back in London, she was ready to prove it. She was having a late birthday celebration at her barn in Sussex and asked Paul if he wanted to come. It felt like a good way for him to meet all of the most important people in her life.

Everyone remembers how much fun the evening was. The guest list—which stretched to nearly a hundred people—was incredibly varied. There were people connected to dozens of Heather's key charities, as well as people from her gym, her neighbors and old friends from Britain and abroad. In the middle of them, Paul mingled like everyone else. He and Heather danced closely and felt fantastic. Best of all, Heather's friends respected their privacy. None went to the press after the party, even though they could probably have made big money by revealing details of the relationship.

Keeping out of the public eye hadn't been easy, but it had been surprisingly fun. Heather and Paul said it sometimes felt like a game to outwit the press. As the weeks passed and they relaxed even more, they came up with ever more ridiculous code words when they spoke on the phone.

"Hello, Lord Jock of Dundee," Heather would say as she took a call one day. "Nice to hear from you, Mr. Patel," she would say the next. "I need to take this call. It's Vladimir, my Russian masseur," she would say to friends on another. Paul's attempts to match the description with a suitable accent meant they spent the first part of most conversations laughing rather than speaking.

It was a dinner with Ringo Starr and his wife, Barbara Bach, that finally blew Heather and Paul's cover. They were at a restaurant near Paul's London home—a stone's throw from the iconic pedestrian crossing on Abbey Road. A whole bank of photographers seemed to be lined up outside when the foursome emerged and tried to head home. The following day, Paul and Heather tried to lie low. His daughter, Mary, had come to visit with her new son, Arthur, and, after ensuring there were no photographers or reporters around, all four headed off to play in the park. They weren't on their own for long. But Heather was amazed to see that Paul didn't care.

He had spotted a lone photographer as she and Paul took a break on a park bench and watched his grandson play. Heather had instinctively withdrawn her arm from his. She was still desperate to stop the gossips. But Paul pulled her back close.

"Don't worry about it," he whispered. Then, with a quick smile at Mary, he got up and walked over to the photographer. By the time he got there, a reporter had emerged as well. Heather flashed a look at Mary. Neither of them knew what Paul was going to do.

From her park bench it was hard to hear exactly what Paul was saying. He told Heather later that he simply asked what the photographer wanted. "A picture of you two together," he was told, as the photographer looked over at Heather. Paul agreed—on the condition that they would then be left alone. The reporter jumped forward as the photograph was taken. He asked Paul about his relationship with Heather. She smiled, convinced he would reply with a simple "no comment." But he didn't.

"We've grown close. We're very good friends. She is a very impressive woman. We are an item," he said, throwing off the cloak of secrecy with a flourish. Paul then said something else. "What we don't need at this stage is photographers lurking in the bushes. If this is to develop, then give us a chance. I'm not a politician and we are not spies. I don't want to be surrounded by photographers because that could wreck something." This short and dignified statement was printed in full in almost every newspaper the next day. But not one of them took the slightest bit of notice of the message.

Heather found herself under siege from that moment on. She had been a public figure before, but this was something entirely different. What she couldn't believe was the relentless nature of the press hounding. Photographers and reporters were outside every door. They were at her home, her offices and everywhere in between. The reporters seemed to call everyone she had ever met—or anyone they thought she might have ever met. Every detail of her life suddenly seemed important to them. A photograph of her leaving her gym seemed to be more important than one of the Prime Minister signing a peace agreement in Northern Ireland. The whole world seemed to have gone upside down.

Heather thought of all the days she had been desperate to attract the media's attention about the landmines in Croatia, the mutilated children in Sierra Leone or the orphans in Cambodia. So often it had seemed as if no one was available to speak to her. The newspapers' budgets seemed too low to put anyone on the stories. Now she knew what the papers were really spending their time and money doing. They were hounding celebrities and paying big money for any supposed dirt they could dig up on them. It just seemed a tragic waste of resources.

The press attention could also be frightening. Less than three years after Princess Diana's death, Heather learned firsthand that photographers still chased their targets in cars. They still blocked sidewalks, climbed over walls and intruded on private land. And all for a few grainy shots of a woman they had so often snubbed in the past. Heather's final worry back then was her safety at home. The newspapers didn't seem to have any reservations about telling their readers exactly where she lived. When she was there alone at night, she started to worry if anyone might be outside her windows. Her isolated barn had long been her dream home. Now it seemed a dangerous liability.

While Heather felt as if she was being beaten up by the media, Paul seemed suddenly relieved that their secret romance was out in the open. For the first time since they had met, their lives were no longer exactly in synch. People who knew him well said Paul had been transformed in the past few months. Reporter Dominic Mohan remembers seeing Paul in the early autumn of 1999 and then in the spring of 2000.

"The sparkle is clearly back in his eyes. He is having fun again, laughing like a man reborn," Dominic said after their second meeting. When he spoke to Paul about a possible interview, Dominic passed on his thoughts. Paul said he couldn't have agreed with them more. Aware that he was treading on very sensitive ground, Dominic asked further questions about how Paul was coping with widowhood, and about his hopes for the future. Paul couldn't have been more open in his replies.

"I feel better now," he agreed. "I thought it would take as long as it takes to get through the grief—a long time. I thought, *how long would Linda want me to take to get over it, to be down? A month? Maybe two?* Once you get to three or four months, she would have been: 'Come on, snap out of it, get on with your life!' That gave me the feeling it was OK to smile again. My lasting memory of her is just her rock 'n' roll spirit, really. People expect to see me taking life in a serious way. But that's not what Linda would have wanted. It's not how I feel."

In private, Paul told close friends that he was convinced that Heather was the only woman who could have lifted his sprits so completely. "You can't help when you fall in love. When it happens, it happens," he said. "I've got romance back in my life. I love her. We spend as much time as we can together and it is not purely platonic." Saying all this in private was one thing, but Paul was about to spring yet another surprise on Heather. He was going to say it in public as well—on national television.

The situation was the extraordinarily public accolade that Heather was granted because of her charitable work. She was being featured in a schmaltzy and now forgotten Sunday night television format called *Stars and Their Lives*.

"She is gorgeous, but she is gutsy. She is the model who became a model campaigner, the beauty who battles against the bad times. Ladies and gentlemen, she is Heather Mills," said presenter Carol Vorderman at the start of the show.

As well as several of Heather's oldest friends, some high profile supporters including Richard Branson, the Duchess of Kent and the boxer Chris Eubank were all happy to appear in their friend's support. But Heather knew for certain that one person would not be appearing on camera. Despite the huge public interest in the relationship, she wanted Paul to stay firmly in the wings. She was still acutely sensitive to the way his family might feel if the relationship got too high profile. And she wanted the evening's focus to be on her charities. Most were getting great exposure and she hoped extra funds might come flooding in when viewers saw how much good they did.

But 15 minutes into the show, the atmosphere in the studio became electric. Paul was striding towards the set with a huge grin on his face. The applause was deafening.

"We know that you very much like to keep your private life exactly that—private," Carol said to a shocked Heather. "You've never been seen on television together. But unknown to you, Sir Paul McCartney said, 'Can I please come on her program?' so here he is."

Heather shook her head in disbelief as Paul reached out to hold her hand. She carried on smiling as he carried on surprising her. Not only was he appearing with her, he wanted to tell the world how they had met and what he thought of her.

"When I saw her I thought, *Wow, she looks great.* A very beautiful, true, fine woman. That was the first impression and, then, when I heard her speak, I was very impressed. So I found her phone number—like you do—and rang her up and said, 'We should talk about some charity stuff and I like what you're doing.' So we had three or four meetings, all very prim and proper, then she came to my office to talk about the charity and I realized that I fancied her."

The pair carried on talking, almost oblivious to the cameras. Then Heather heard herself say it. "I love him," she muttered to Carol as Paul began another anecdote and the studio erupted in laughter.

"On national telly?" interrupted Paul.

"You started it. I was going to say nothing about you tonight," she replied to even more laughter.

"And can I ask you the same question?" Carol said, turning to Paul. He didn't miss a beat.

"Yeah, I love her, too," he said.

The audience loved it.

"Paul looked as besotted as man can be without having to

display a 'Do Not Disturb' sign," was how one audience member put it. As they were driven home after the taping, Heather and Paul both knew another milestone had been crossed. It was a wonderful, happy time for them both—even more so because it was all so unexpected. But behind the scenes there was already much more to their relationship than simple fun and games. Far from prying eyes, black clouds had been gathering for some time. Heather and Paul's love affair was being tested from the very start.

Heather can't forget the first time Sir Paul cried in front of her. They were out walking at his country estate less than a month after their tentative relationship had begun. They had been talking about Linda. Unsure of how to deal with the situation, Heather kept looking ahead, stealing only the occasional glance at Paul to check if he was OK. She already knew how strong and proud he was. She knew he wouldn't want her to make a fuss. She knew he still needed to grieve and she was proud he could open up to her so completely.

Those tears weren't the last either of them would shed as their love affair got underway. Paul cried almost every day for the first six months of the relationship. His memories of Linda cast deep shadows. Heather tried to give him the space he needed to come to terms with his loss and his new life. She tried to spot what might remind him of his late wife so she could be ready to comfort him if he needed it. And she knew when she needed to go to another room and leave him in peace with his thoughts.

Ironically, as Paul's clouds gradually lifted and he began to smile more than he cried, Heather's life was to take a turn for the worse. Two of her closest friends were seriously ill. In the late winter and early spring of 2000, both of them would die.

The first shock came when Heather's old friend, Sabrina, found her breast cancer had returned. The pair had met years earlier in the gym, just before Sabrina had a mastectomy. Sabrina had been one of the few people Heather had told about Paul in the early days of their relationship. She knew her friend, a former journalist, could give her advice on dealing with press interest. After so many years in remission, everyone had hoped Sabrina's future was assured. But when the cancer came back, it grew fast. Sabrina died within weeks of her new diagnosis.

As she grieved for her friend—and offered to help her teenage son and his family—Heather had another crisis to face. Sam had been just sixteen when Heather had first met her in the cancer ward of the Middlesex Hospital. Visiting her had been particularly tough. It was the first time Heather had been back to that particular hospital since her mother had died there just before her wedding in 1989.

Sam had fought cancer for two harsh years, and Heather had tried to take her mind off it with a series of fun days out when her health had allowed. Just after Sabrina's death, Sam too slipped away. Heather spoke at the young girl's funeral. She had rarely felt so vulnerable, and could hardly have been more grateful to Paul for offering support when she needed it the most.

Anger about the injustice of the world kept Heather going though the low months of 2000. As usual, she decided to blank out all the distractions in her life by focusing on people who were going through a lot worse. Paul talks of a quiet afternoon they were spending at Heather's home as the media storm blew around them. A man had been given Heather's number at his local hospital and he called for help after his son lost a leg in a motorcycle accident.

"I only got one end of the conversation, but I could tell the man was being saved. Hearing someone giving help to other people who are in need has got to change your life," Paul told friends afterwards.

What he also learned was that his beautiful new girlfriend was the toughest of task-masters. "I see myself as an antidote to doctors and nurses," she told him. "The medical profession has to be cautious, but I can go in and say that nothing is impossible. I saw a little lad who had lost a leg and he so wanted to play football. I told him, 'Wow, you're going to be a bionic man. Like

Robocop. You'll fly with that artificial leg.' And we all saw him start smiling again."

With adults, Paul saw Heather get even tougher. "It's all psychological. I want to get rid of that lazy, dependency attitude. Doctors are afraid to give their patients a kick up the backside, but I'm tough. I say to the parents of amputees, 'Look, if you put in a kid's mind and say he can't do something then he won't. If you say the sky's the limit, he'll try anything. However hard it is, you need to push him forward so he doesn't give up.'" And what was so clear to Paul was that Heather was speaking from experience.

With this in mind, it should have been no surprise when she took him to task on the first charitable venture they carried out together. It was for the fund-raising single "Voice"—and the behind-the-scenes story of its production still makes the studio staff smile. Heather had written the song to raise money for disability charities and to get the message across that disabled people deserved their voice. She planned to record it in a Greek studio where her sister was working. To Fiona's immense relief, Heather agreed to talk through the lyrics rather than singing them. But they wanted someone to sing the backing track. Paul immediately offered his services.

If he had expected an easy ride, he was in for a shock. Heather proved to be a demanding and fearless producer. The studio staff, star-struck from the moment Sir Paul arrived, said they couldn't believe that she kept telling him to do another take. She would listen to the playbacks then ask—or more accurately tell—Paul to do the track differently. "Sing that part a bit higher, Paul," she would demand.

"Do it again, but like this," she said. "One more time, but like I said at the beginning," she instructed.

Amazingly, Paul, the richest man in British music and the author of some of the world's most recorded songs, was always happy to oblige. Everyone had a great time working on the single. But it was easy to see why when Paul had to find one word to describe his new girlfriend it was "bossy."

He could also have used the word "busy"—because keeping up with Heather's workload was an exhausting business. At the end of 2000, they waited nervously for news from the country that had first brought them together: Sierra Leone. Out in Africa, the machetes of the Revolutionary United Front were still hacking off the limbs of so many children. And still the world pretty much looked the other way.

Once more, Heather was hugely frustrated that so few people wanted to cover this humanitarian crisis. Her normal belief was that as long as there was a human angle to a story then it would get the papers interested. But what could be more human than a six-year-old girl whose hands had been cut off after she had seen her parents die? In December, Heather was preparing to fly out to the country to re-open an orphanage in the town of Makeni. She had also been given the use of two properties in Freetown, the capital, for limb replacements. She wanted to see if visiting them would finally get the media interested. But before she could finalize the plans, she got a call to see if she and Paul could help with a secret mercy mission called Operation Orphan.

The call was from Hope and Homes for Children, a British charity that cares for child victims of wars and natural disasters. For two years, its staff had been caring for a group of orphans in Sierra Leone evicted from their safe house and forced to live deep in rebel territory in the bush. Every day, the children had been under siege—the girls at risk of being snatched as sex slaves, the boys as child soldiers. By late 2000, even the countryside was deemed unsafe and around 100 children were being moved towards Freetown. Hope and Homes for Children director James Whiting desperately needed a safe house for them when they arrived. He called Heather and she freed up space in the properties she was using for limb-replacements. These could be the refuges the children needed. But would they survive the journey?

James and his charity workers had divided the children into six groups which traveled some 75 miles by truck, ferry and on foot through jungle trails. Some were as young as three years old and many were seriously ill. The first five groups were welcomed into the first big property Heather had provided—which was dubbed Heather House by the locals. But the sixth had not arrived. Back in England, Heather and Paul paced up and down desperately waiting for news. Both knew the risks these children were facing as they walked through mine-strewn, rebel territory. Both were euphoric when the call came through saying the final 16 kids had made it unharmed.

Having introduced Paul to so many of her own important causes, Heather knew it was only fair for her to take on some of his. She and VIVA's Juliet Gellatley were well on their way to becoming firm friends, and Heather started reading up on animal welfare and food production. She also modified her own diet. Paul gave her his philosophy on food and she had to agree it produced good results. A few eyebrows had probably been raised by the 25-year age gap between them, but a lifetime of healthy eating meant Paul certainly didn't look his age.

"He's so sweet, he's energizing," Heather said when she was asked about the age gap. "He's like a little Peter Pan character. When you see him walking down the street, he literally skips, just like a little boy. In many ways he is definitely the youngest guy I have ever been out with."

As the weeks and months passed, Heather and Paul's relationship grew stronger. The press intrusion continued and Heather was starting to worry that her charities were starting to get overshadowed. But she was so happy in her private life that she allowed herself to believe it would all come right in the end. She thought back to the other men who had been in her life. All had somehow sought to control her or hold her back. Paul seemed confident enough to set her free. By the end of 2000, she was also convinced they could achieve great things together—and this meant as much to her as anything.

"Psychologically, I feel on an equal level with Paul. There are a million reasons why I love him, but the main one is that I'm with someone who is totally secure in who he is and doesn't resent my work. We are together seven days a week. We sit down and go through our calendars together each month and we don't do anything if it takes us away from each other. The best thing is that Paul fell in love with who I am and he wouldn't try to change me. Just as I wouldn't dream of telling him to stop singing and painting and touring, he wouldn't try and stop my charity work. This is what my life is about."

In January 2001, Paul was a man with a mission. He wanted to buy an engagement ring. He and Heather were having the most romantic of holidays in India. They went to the extraordinarily beautiful pink city of Jaipur in Rajasthan. They toured around the beaches of Goa and spent Heather's 33rd birthday on the glorious Palace on Wheels—the train dubbed India's Orient Express. Heather remembers lying in their cabin at midnight, a full moon outside, watching as they rattled through the amazing countryside. She and Paul did seem to travel well together. Far from the pressures of day-to-day life, they simply talked and dreamed and relaxed. In private, Paul could just be the boy from Liverpool, Heather the ordinary girl from Newcastle. Heather was now well aware that the McCartney family loved its long heritage of in-jokes, comic phrases and silly stories. She was thrilled that she and Paul were steadily building up a new repertoire of their own.

As they flew back to London, Heather didn't know that Paul had one more reason for smiling that year. He had found the perfect ring—a mix of sapphires and diamonds he had seen in Rajasthan. All he had to do now was decide when and where to propose.

Unfortunately, romance went right off the agenda the moment the pair got back to London. An earthquake had hit India within hours of leaving the country, and the early news reports spoke of thousands of dead and injured. What Heather knew from grim experience was that the injured would include a huge number of amputees. She and Paul sat in shock watching the television coverage. The latest figures talked of at least 30,000 casualties and an equal number of serious injuries. Both of them had loved India. But realistically they knew that its rural areas would be ill-equipped to deal with this kind of natural disaster. The country would need help. Heather was prepared to give it.

"I need to go back out there," she told Paul. "We need to start raising money."

She hit the phones to try and find out exactly how bad the situation was and exactly what kind of help was required. One aid agency told her that while the number of new amputees injured in the earthquake was likely to run easily into four figures they would only be adding to a far larger pool of limbless adults and children. Too few of these people were getting artificial limbs as it was. The earthquake would only lengthen the waiting lists and condemn even more people to immobile, unproductive lives. Or at least it would unless Heather had her way.

She took a deep breath and rang up some of the newspapers and magazines which had been making her life a misery for the past 18 months. "They've had people and money to spare chasing me. Let's see if they can find the same to help earthquake victims," she said to Paul.

The results weren't that inspiring. One of the few publications willing to help was *Hello* magazine, the glossy title which had always been supportive of Heather. Most of the tabloids that were hounding her didn't even bother to return her calls. But the deal Heather signed with *Hello* provided enough money to help replace up to 5,000 limbs and would be a great starting point for her campaign. Paul watched his girlfriend in amazement as she galvanized supporters for this new cause. Her energy was infectious. Her "bossiness" got results. He knew he was right to have bought her a ring—but he was worried that an Indian earthquake zone might be too dangerous even for her. She soon put him straight.

"He was worried about the water and the disease, but he realized that wasn't going to stop me," she told friends. "He knew what he took on when he met me, and he is as supportive as any partner could be. He is very encouraging, and I am pretty tough."

As if to prove it, less than two months after returning from India, Heather flew back to see the recovery efforts first-hand. She was traveling with award-winning photographer Ken Lennox and was ready to pitch in and help wherever required. With no hotels to stay in, they were ready to sleep in tents. And with severe road and rail damage, they were prepared to travel by bike if that was what it took to get around.

Their first stop was at the Red Cross Hospital in the Gujarat Province town of Bhuj, one of the worst hit areas of the quake. One of the patients she met was little Dilip Pranji, a ten-year-old boy whose left arm had been severed when a piece of farm machinery fell on him during the first of the quake's aftershocks.

The hospital doctors were mainly aid workers from Scandinavia. They remember how gentle Heather was with Dilip and how hard she worked to win his confidence. Unable to speak his language and with no translator on hand, she simply sat on his bed, stroked his hair and smiled. Then she took the boy's hand and placed it on her own artificial leg. As his face fell in surprise, she unclipped the limb to prove that she too was an amputee. The moment was as powerful in India as it had been all those years ago in Zagreb, Croatia. It made people feel less alone and proved to them that they had hope.

The hospital in Bhuj was like a city of tents. The Red Cross had set up outdoor wards to cope with the recent arrivals and replace the damaged buildings. As Heather went from tent to tent, the doctors remember hearing peals of laughter ring out as she repeated her party trick with more and more amputees. That wasn't all she did. The following day, in a different hospital some 40 miles away, she met a five-year-old boy known only as Vikas. He had lost both legs and had been trapped in the hospital for five weeks. Heather tried to cheer him up by tickling him and playing tricks with her leg, but he didn't even smile. Through an interpreter, he told Heather he missed the sunshine. So she clipped her leg back on, picked him up and carried him out for a few moments of fresh air. It was the kind of instinctive, practical caring that hadn't been seen since Princess Diana's death. It was proof that the power of touch shouldn't ever be underestimated.

One of the most important stops on Heather's schedule was the Jaipur Limb Clinic. It fits artificial limbs for amputees and had been overwhelmed since the earthquake. Heather talked to its staff, worked out its needs and set a fund-raising target to help up to 8,000 people get false limbs. The total would help around 1,500 people who had suffered amputations in the earthquake, and 6,500 others who were already on the waiting lists.

"I'll do whatever it takes," she said back in London. So she kicked off the process by giving a rare interview to one of her despised tabloids in return for a sizeable donation. Then she got back on the phones to organize even more help. It is easy to underestimate how much effort she put into this particular campaign. And it proved an important point about her. All those who would one day call Heather a ruthless gold digger should ask why, with one of the world's richest men at her side, she would still work so hard to help others. The truth is she still wanted to lead by example. Getting cash from Paul wouldn't encourage others to get involved. Somehow she knew that doing good means getting your hands dirty. She would never be above that challenge.

As if to prove it, Heather and Paul were about to join forces for another major charitable campaign. The issue of landmines had effectively brought them together and Paul had been horrified at the statistics that Heather could reel off almost in her sleep. She told of the 60 million mines that are believed to be buried in some 70 countries, of the 26,000 people including 12,000 children who are killed or injured by landmines every year. And of the new killing fields that are laid whenever new conflicts spring up around the globe. They talked of the work they could do in Afghanistan, Bosnia, Cambodia and Mozambique to try and alleviate local suffering, and of the lobbying and campaigning they could do to try and stop the manufacture and distribution of these dirtiest of bombs.

As part of this, they both became passionate supporters of the Adopt-A-Minefield charity in America. They had been told about it by John and Jodie Eastman, Linda McCartney's brother and sister-in-law. Jodie had introduced Heather to one of the charity's founders at an informal lunch and triggered a detailed discussion about land clearance as well as survivor assistance. Heather and Paul decided to become goodwill ambassadors for Adopt-A-Minefield in the U.S. and prepared to set up a U.K. version as well. As part of this new launch, Heather agreed to return to Croatia to film a new 25-minute documentary about the amputees there. It was sobering stuff—and having effectively flown straight from the natural disaster in India to the man-made disaster in the Balkans, she says she couldn't decide which was more depressing.

Paul agreed to do the commentary for the documentary and it was launched at a reception at London's Piccadilly Circus in June 2001.

"Imagine living in a country during a terrible war and then peace is declared," Paul said on the program. "You think the killing is over, but when you take your kids to the beach, you can't walk on it because your children could get blown up. This is the legacy of the land mine. Land mines take or wreck three lives an hour, every hour of every day of every year. We have to come together now to try and stop that."

When he talked to reporters after the documentary had been shown, Paul's words were interesting in a slightly different way. "It isn't brave to go to war and leave landmines behind," he began. "I don't think any soldier really wants that. Our role is to try to persuade governments that leaving the war behind is a cowardly idea. At the moment, it is up to us at Adopt-A-Minefield to do that clearance, and I don't think it should be."

As he spoke, Heather felt a huge burst of pride. When she heard him say phrases such as "our role" and "up to us," she knew he was connecting himself wholeheartedly with the campaigns that meant the world to her. She gripped his hand a little tighter as they headed home at the end of the evening. She was convinced that she and Paul could stay together, stay happy and make a difference in the world.

By the early summer of 2001, both Heather and Paul were in desperate need of a rest. As well as everything else, Paul had been on a short tour promoting the new greatest hits album from Wings. Heather had been fighting a bizarre battle with a British tabloid newspaper, which wanted to print the address of the new more secure house she had bought in the south coast town of Hove. Meanwhile, both of them were increasingly worried about George Harrison's health and spent a lot of time on the phone talking to him and his wife, Olivia.

Paul suggested a few day's away in England's Lake District, just north of Liverpool, so he and Heather could finally unwind. It is stunningly beautiful Wordsworth and Beatrix Potter country, and the pair had enjoyed an invigorating, private visit the previous year. This time they wanted to go on more long walks and clear their heads for the rest of the year. And Paul felt he had been carrying Heather's engagement ring around for much too long. He was ready to propose.

"I love you, Heather. Will you marry me?"

Paul went down on one knee just before dinner on the first evening of their break.

Heather remembers being too surprised to speak. Paul had to ask again. Then she said "yes." They both cried.

The ring was a huge success. Heather cried again when she realized Paul had bought it six months ago on their trip to India. But she tried to hide it in the hotel restaurant when they finally made it out for their evening meal. She knew the horrors of being a public person, with every aspect of her life in public view. For just one evening she wanted this to be their little secret. Deep inside she knew she needed some calm before the storm.

They decided that they would tell the press when they got back to London. They made some calls from Paul's house in St. John's Wood and the photographers flocked up Abbey Road to get their first photos of the couple—and the ring. In typical fashion, neither Heather nor Paul dressed up for the obligatory photo-call. Paul wore an open-necked blue shirt while Heather wore a simple, black sleeveless top. Paul was a lot keener than Heather to step outside his gates and face the press. He clearly wanted to show off his pretty young fiancée. Heather held back, very much aware that the press did not always react the way you hoped. When they did walk out into the bear's den, the press erupted with noise and requests. Most of Heather's nerves faded away, and things started to feel good. There seemed to be a genuine warmth in the air. *Maybe the papers will lighten up now,* she thought. She even prepared to joke along with them.

"Give her a kiss, Paul!"

"How about a hug, Heather?"

"We don't kiss on demand. It's spontaneous," she called out, laughing, after yet another request. But in reality they didn't need to. Their body language said it all. Friends, fans and strangers could all read it. This was a very happy, very relaxed and very comfortable couple.

"Paul McCartney has always been known for his broad, boyish smile, but the ear-splitting grin he sported while announcing his engagement to Heather Mills was something else entirely. This was the happiest we had seen him since the death of Linda tore his world apart," said veteran music writer Charles Shaar Murray, who has known Paul and followed his career for decades. "He now seems to have another chance of happiness and it would take a real sour square indeed to refrain from wishing him all the best." One of Heather's oldest friends agreed.

"Paul and Heather have both known more than their fair share of grief. They are two people who give of themselves generously and have found that what they both need now is love," said Phillip Goodhand-Tait with a beautiful and entirely accurate turn of phrase. Back inside their house, Heather and Paul did finally kiss. Their trial by media was over. Surely they would now be allowed to plan their wedding in peace?

The second half of 2001 should have been the happiest time in Heather and Paul's lives. But tragedies were to stalk them at almost every turn. There would be huge highs for Heather as she celebrated her engagement with friends and family and collected an extraordinary fund-raising honor in the United States. But there would be awful lows as well.

She and Paul took a month-long break from the world after announcing their engagement to try and recharge their batteries. Behind the scenes, they were thrilled at how well the U.K. version of the Adopt-A-Minefield charity was being received. Brits seemed to like its clear, practical mission statement: to physically clear land of mines, one square meter at a time. And in America the message had also been heard loud and clear.

In New York on September 10, 2001, Heather stood proudly alongside Hillary Clinton and Sarah Ferguson at a charity awards reception. She was being honored for her global land-mines work. She remembers how much everyone laughed back stage when Paul played the fool to try and take everyone's minds off their nerves.

But then, of course, came September 11th.

Heather and Paul were on the tarmac at JFK when the planes hit the Twin Towers. Like everyone else, they sat scared and confused as the first sketchy reports came in about the nature of the attack. Heather remembers spending the next three days glued to the television in a Manhattan hotel.

She and Paul had always loved America. If it was under attack, then they felt the call to join its defense. And they were determined to do whatever they could to help the victims of that terrible day. Paul wrote a song, "Freedom," and helped arrange the massive star-studded benefit concert at Madison Square Garden. Heather made sure that as many people as possible would have the chance to experience it. She personally handed out tickets to fire department staff and other relief workers at Ground Zero. They raised some $40 million for the firefighters' families and a host of other related causes. On stage with a line of firefighters at the concert finale, Paul felt the tears start to flow. He thought of his own father, Jim, who had been a volunteer firefighter in Liverpool during the Second World War. Paul felt as if he was honoring him as well as all of the September 11th heroes that night. It felt right to be doing it in New York, the city which had always seemed so closely associated with John Lennon.

Less than three weeks after the concert there was more fear, confusion and sadness when Heather and Paul flew back to New York yet again to see George Harrison—it would turn out to be the last time they did. His health was fading away and they took the Concorde to ensure they reached him as fast as possible. As they approached JFK, they flew over the black clouds of smoke that were rising from Queens. American Airlines Flight 587 had crashed there in an accident that everyone initially feared was another terrorist atrocity.

George died two weeks after their final visit and Paul and Heather held a silent tribute for yet another close friend they had lost. They realized, soberly, that they had attended more funerals than weddings during their relationship. There had been more deaths among their friends than births.

Both vowed to work harder at living in the moment to fight off these dark shadows. For all the sadness in their world, they needed to remember that when they were alone together or spending time with their families and friends, they were happy. Up in Liverpool, they threw themselves into the McCartney clan's New Year celebrations with even more abandon. Then they headed back to India for Heather's 34th birthday. Paul gave her the matching sapphire and diamond bracelet he had bought alongside her engagement ring and had been keeping for exactly a year. They felt like the luckiest, happiest couple in the world. They set their hearts upon a summer wedding.

"If you wouldn't wear your dog ... please don't wear any fur."

—Heather Mills McCartney

The only difference between your "best friend" and animals killed for their fur is how we treat them. All animals feel pain and suffer when trappers and farmers break their necks or electrocute them for their pelts. **Learn more at PETA.org.**

HEATHER MILLS McCARTNEY POSES FOR AN AD CAMPAIGN FOR PETA.

In 2005, the *NY Post* reported, "McCartney marched across Sixth Ave. with an army of camera crews and stormed the offices of Sweetface, J.Lo's fur-trimmed clothing line, to present the singer-actress with a grisly PETA video showing innocent mammals being skinned alive."

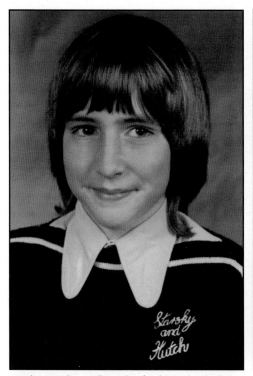

A shy Heather Mills smiles for her school photograph aged 12, sporting a fetching Starsky and Hutch sweater.

Paul McCartney and Heather Mills.

Paul McCartney and Heather Mills meet up to share custody of their daughter Beatrice.